*Sheila has a gift. She is inte* ——— *she can write. I encourage you to unpackage her gift by reading this book.*
Rev. Terry Dorey
Pastor of Church Ministries at Parkdale Baptist Church

*Sheila is a breath of fresh air! Her opinions are researched, fact-based, and dotted with emotion just to make it real. A talk with her is something to really look forward to; it is time well spent.*
Janice Rowe
Mother of four

*Monday nights at our house involve eating together as a family and always reading the Intel to find out what Sheila has to say this week. I find her articles always to be insightful and thought-provoking, and she always gives my wife and I a laugh.*
Bruce Mackay
Mackay Insurance Brokers Inc.

*I just wanted to write you a note to say how much I enjoy reading your columns in the weekly paper. I have found that even though I don't always agree with your opinions, I always find your column thought-provoking and challenging to my own beliefs/opinions.*
Wendy Sparling

*Please keep up the good work you do in your column—you are truly a lodestone of traditional morality in a misaligned GPS world!*
Ken Dowsett

*Sheila is a gifted and inspirational writer who leaves you thinking.*
C. Kelly

*I really enjoy your work in the Intel. I can relate to every-thing you're writing about—having two young kids myself! Kids screaming in the store...potty training...good stuff!*
Sean Kelly
MIX 97 Director of Programming/Morning Host

*I am an avid fan of your column in the Intelligencer and never miss it. I know that even before finishing your article I will have a smile on my face and my heart will be lighter! Please keep on writing—it is valuable to all of us who just can't seem to put the everyday, ordinary nuances of life into such a clear picture with words.*
Debby Nunes

*I enjoy your column every Monday in the Intelligencer, as do many of my grandmother friends. You have a real gift for providing good info with a nice touch of humour.*
Margaret McIntosh
Grandma

*Sheila's column offers sound parenting advice that is both workable and achievable. There's none of the fad psychology that is so prevalent today. Good stuff.*
Al Baker
DJ, UCB 102.3

*I enjoy your columns in the Belleville Intelligencer very much. I read it every week... I really appreciate your sense of humour...Thanks for sharing your experiences; it's nice to know others have home lives as crazy as mine (and I wouldn't have it any other way).*
Brigette Crowley

*I always enjoy Sheila's columns; she writes with purpose, integrity and inevitably makes me smile. Well done, Sheila!"*
Marie Kelly

_Happy reading!_

_Sheila Gregoire_

# reality check

## sheila wray gregoire

Essance

PUBLISHING

Belleville, Ontario, Canada

# Reality Check

## Copyright © 2004, Sheila Wray Gregoire

ISBN: 1-55306-918-8

**For more information or
to order additional copies, please contact:**

www.SheilaWrayGregoire.com

or

Sheila Wray Gregoire
Box 20201
Belleville, ON  Canada
K8N 5V1

*Essence Publishing* is a Christian Book Publisher dedicated to fur-
thering the work of Christ through the written word. For more information, contact:
20 Hanna Court, Belleville, Ontario, Canada K8P 5J2.
Phone: 1-800-238-6376 • Fax: (613) 962-3055.
E-mail: publishing@essencegroup.com
Internet: www.essencegroup.com

*To Rebecca and Katie,*
*who fill my days with laughter, love, and hugs.*

*And to Christopher,*
*my precious baby who changed my life.*
*You are always close to my heart.*

# *Table of Contents*

# *Tidbits*

# Acknowledgements

First and foremost, my thanks to Sarah MacWhirter, the former editor of the *Belleville Intelligencer*, to Linda O'Connor, the Lifestyles editor, and to Paul Varga in Penticton, all of whom took a chance on me. I'm having such fun, and I thank you for giving me this forum.

Thanks to my family, who keep cropping up in these columns unawares and who don't seem to mind. Special thanks to Keith, who is usually the brunt of my jokes. I do love you so.

My girls are great fun and give me plenty of fodder. So does my extended family, and especially my father-in-law. A friend once said to him, "When you die, she'll have nothing left to write about." So thanks, Dad.

I also want to acknowledge the DJs at Mix 97 and UCB 102.3 in Belleville for reading me on the air occasionally and starting the conversation about many of my columns. So thanks to Sean Kelly, Joey Martin, Bruce MacKay, Al Baker, Dana Rogalsky, and Gary Hoogvliet. I appreciate it.

Most of all, I'd like to thank the readers for the support they give me. I love receiving e-mails from you all, and it's such an incredible feeling to know that I've written something that has touched you. Thank you to all those at Parkdale Baptist Church who encourage me weekly and to others who have sent kind notes. They help keep me going.

Finally, my mother was the first one who taught me about parenting. Mom, you showed me such incredible love, and I hope I can inspire others to do the same for their kids. And to my perfect Father, my God who has carried me through heartache and turned much sorrow into joy, thank you for this chance to write. I pray I may always encourage others as you have encouraged me.

# *Introduction*

Some people have a lot of friends, a lot of pets, a lot of clothes, or a lot of coupons for Tim Hortons' coffee. I seem to have a lot of opinions, and as you read this book you'll become intimately acquainted with them. Every week I share an insight I've had about parenting, marriage, or family, and this collection of columns represents the best of the first two years of that effort. Many people have told me that they don't always agree with what I write, but they like reading it anyway. My columns make them think. That's one of the best compliments I can receive. So whether or not you agree with everything in this book, I hope you find it fun, interesting, and thought-provoking. And I hope some of it makes you laugh!

These began appearing in the *Belleville Intelligencer* in August of 2002 and in the *Southern Exposure* in Penticton in February of 2003. In them, I write frequently about my kids, since they're my guinea pigs for my parenting ideas. I think you might understand the columns better if you understand my family situation, so here goes. Rebecca's 9, and Katie's 7. Our son Christopher was born between them and lived just one month. I talk about all three quite regularly.

My husband's a pediatrician in Belleville, and sometimes what I write is inspired by conversations we have about how to deal with the problems that walk into his office.

My mother is a career woman, a knitter, and a great parent. She raised me alone, and she, too, factors into many of my discussions.

My father-in-law is a rabid Detroit Red Wings fan. When the Red Wings won the Stanley Cup a couple of years back, the *Intelligencer* took a picture of him out on his lawn with his replica Stanley Cup and all his Red Wings gear. Whenever something about the Red Wings makes it into a column, he hears about it for weeks. So that's why they're mentioned so much. I think he likes it.

My mother-in-law is a wonderful grandma. She does crafts, she bakes, she has lots of Santas, and she always has chocolate on hand for the kids.

As you read these columns, you'll get to know these people, as well as my views on school, childhood illness, ADD, lizards, feeding kids, keeping teens on track, and the Children's Aid Society. What you see in this book is what was in the paper, with the exception of some glaring grammatical errors that I have since corrected.

My goal in writing these has always been to encourage and motivate us to do the best job we can at the most important job we have: parenting. Whether those years are behind you or you're in the midst of diapers, school buses, or acne, I hope you will enjoy these columns as they make you think, make you laugh, and sometimes even make you cry.

— *Sheila Gregoire,*
*October 4, 2004*
*Belleville, Ontario*

# *P*arenting Foibles

Parenting causes lots of worries, grey hairs, and sleepless nights. But it also brings big laughs. Some days, you just look at yourself in the mirror and say, "I can't believe I'm doing this." As parents, we all do things we would never in our right minds do otherwise. Yet somehow, when you've got kids, it all seems perfectly natural. See if you can relate.

## Are We There Yet?
*This column was first published August 19, 2002*

*I*t's that time of year again: camping, cottages, water-skiing, boating, and beaches all beckon us. Unfortunately, they all involve a particularly gruesome form of self-torture: car trips with children.

For those of us travelling this summer to fun-filled destinations where we can relax, getting there can be an exercise in frustration. Tiny ones repeatedly bleat "are we there yet?" while older ones yell, over and over, "she's on my side of the seat!" How can we survive this nightmare?

Every summer, our family takes an eight-hour trip down to

Pennsylvania and a three-hour one up to Muskoka. They're not always pleasant, but we've found some ways to pass the time, many gleaned from other parents who have trod this path before us.

First, you must have a zero tolerance for fighting. My award for "Shrewdest Mother of the Year" goes to a mom with two girls who told them they were going to visit Grandma, some six hours away. She packed their bags, loaded the van, kissed Daddy goodbye, and took off, with a stern warning that when the first fight broke out she would turn the van around and head home.

> Like that mother, I can't stand fighting or whining in the car.

They made it about half an hour before she kept her promise, landing them once again in their driveway. The two girls were too stunned even to cry. When they realized this was for real, they sobbed and begged, but their mother would not relent.

A week later, after many promises, they set out again. This time, they made it the whole way. What the girls didn't know was that Mother's vacation time was actually booked for that second week. She knew they wouldn't make it to Grandma's on the first attempt. That was only a trial run to make the point.

Like that mother, I can't stand fighting or whining in the car. It infuriates me, and if I have to listen to that for eight hours, I'm not going. The girls know that, because at the first sign of whining we stop the car.

We've also played every game in the book to keep them occupied: look for all the provincial and state licence plates, count the cows, and find things beginning with all the letters of the alphabet. These really do entertain younger children, though unfortunately they're not the most entertaining for us adults. Coming up with a word for *X*, though, took a lot of brainpower last year. I'm better prepared this year. I'll be on the lookout for a xenolith—a type of rock fragment—as we traverse through the Canadian Shield to Muskoka.

Last year, in a spurt of energy between packing the camper and doing laundry, I laminated some "picture" bingo cards, with horses, cows, railway crossings, signs, and other landmarks. These were big hits, and best of all, the kids did them themselves, so Keith and I had time to talk to each other.

But the smartest thing we ever did was to borrow audio tapes from the library. You can borrow whole books on tape, like *Charlotte's Web* or C.S. Lewis's *Narnia* chronicles. Even ones that aren't as "classic" but that kids still love, like *Magic Tree House* or *Junie B. Jones*, are usually available. Many of them are entertaining for adults, too, and best of all, a lot of them last hours! Hours of not hearing "are we there yet?" but only "it's not over yet, is it?"

I'll leave you with my favourite summer-car-ride story. During a cross-country trip, one eight-year-old girl started to feel very carsick. She rolled the window down, but it didn't seem to help. Her eleven-year-old brother watched her with growing concern as she turned different shades of green. Then, when it was obvious something REALLY BAD was about to happen, he showed tremendous forethought. Sticking out his hands, he caught his sister's vomit and threw it out the window, so that they wouldn't have to sit in a stinky car for the next few days.

So as you're driving to the cottage, and the air conditioning isn't working, and the kids are whining, just be thankful that at least you don't have to catch the vomit.

*This was the first column I ever published. My father-in-law thought I talked about vomit too much. But then, as he soon learned, this would be a common theme in many columns. And in my life.*

## The Great Costume Hunt
*This column was first published October 28, 2002*

*I*'m starting to panic. It's three days before Halloween, and I have yet to buy costumes for my children.

This is a pattern that's repeated every year in our house, as I try to convince my kids to use some of their dress-up clothes to be princesses, yet again. They're not buying it this time. But I just can't get up the enthusiasm to buy two $30 costumes so my children can go and collect $15 worth of candy in the rain while my husband stays behind and passes out $20 worth of candy to other people's kids. Why can't we just turn off all the lights, stand in the shower fully clothed, and let our kids stuff themselves on our own candy? The atmosphere's the same, but it's a lot easier.

I suppose I'm a spoilsport, but even as a child I didn't like Halloween. Trying to come up with a costume that none of the other kids would laugh at seemed a near impossibility. I remember the year I went as Wonder Woman. I loved that costume. But though my plastic bracelets could repel bullets, they couldn't repel the snickers of the those evil fiends in my grade-three class.

Finding a costume involves, first and foremost, finding something that will not label your kids "The Biggest Dorks of All Time." But lack of dorkiness is not the only criteria. I hate dressing kids up as horrid little creatures. Enough of them act horridly already, and there's no reason to give them any incentive to do so even more. Besides, why take the opportunity to glorify gore when you can glorify good? I loved the movement last year, after 9/11, to dress kids up as firefighters and police officers. I wish there were something similar this year. Instead, I'm stuck with a criteria list of *hip*, *cute*, and *kind*, but nothing comes quickly to mind to fit the bill.

But it doesn't stop there. I don't know if anyone else has noticed, but October 31 is remarkably close to November, and November is just plain awful. It's cold, and it rains. So kids have to wear sweatsuits under-neath their costumes, which makes them look like little Pillsbury doughboys, even if they're trying to be bal-lerinas. So let's add *warm* to our list of criteria.

Even assuming I find such a costume, I then have to persuade my girls to do the very thing they've been dreaming of: actually go door to door. Three years ago, when Katie was only three, one family on our street laid coffins out on their lawn and broadcast bone-chilling laughs and screeches throughout our block. The kids were terrified, but we had to pass that house to get to the candy on the other side. So there I was, dragging a terrified Raggedy Ann and a whimpering ballerina past goblins and ghosts and screeches, all so we could collect several tiny Coffee Crisp bars.

But the practical details are not nearly as bad as the pretzels we twist ourselves into trying to overcome parental inconsistencies. All year, we tell kids: Never accept candy from strangers. Don't talk to strangers. Don't go into a stranger's house. And then one night of the year we break all these commandments in one fell swoop! Then we have to lecture our kids yet again to impress upon them that we really did mean those "stranger rules."

For all of you, like me, for whom Halloween seems just too exhausting, there are alternatives. Many malls give out candy, and they're well lit, warm, and there's no rain. Many churches have Halloween parties, so you can avoid the door-to-door altogether and still get enough candy to make kids sick.

But for all these alternatives, you still need costumes. So, like previous years, I will beg or borrow from someone else. And, yes, we'll probably go door to door to our neighbours, simply because I really like them (and because the bone-chilling neighbours have moved away). Then we'll head to the church, where they can bob for apples and get sick some more.

But next year, if you happen to pass my house on Halloween and the lights are out but you hear the shower on, you'll know I've finally had enough.

*I received some of the very first negative e-mails on this one. I wasn't really prepared for it, either, because I didn't think this one was controversial—unlike, say, the spanking one that had just preceded it. But a number of people thought I was a spoilsport and a cheapskate. Maybe so. But my kids have a lot of fun the rest of the year, believe me. I think we parents should all allow ourselves to dread at least some holidays. We are human, after all.*

## Being Stalked by Norwalk
*This column was first published January 27, 2003*

ll over town this morning, far too many sheets, comforters, and blankets are in the washer. And it's not because we had a sudden epiphany about the evils of dust mites, or because we all wanted that spring-fresh scent in the middle of winter. No, it's because our little ones are puking their guts out. Norwalk has come to town.

I hate flu season. My own children have not actually succumbed yet, but I figure it's only a matter of time since we do not actually wash our hands fourteen times a day (or however many times it is that you're supposed to). I remember a few Christmases ago Katie had a terrible stomach virus, and we must have changed her sheets six times in one night. We were down to our last set of bedding (some old sleeping bags I found in the back of the closet), and if she threw up on those we were going to resort to wrapping her in towels. The worst of it was that during the last episode she happened to hit her blankie. And Katie can't sleep without her blankie.

She decided to cuddle with me as a substitute. As a general rule I like cuddling. But I'm not so fond of it if, at any moment, that child may do to my bed what she's already done to hers. Nevertheless, maternal feelings won out that night, and she cuddled; I held my breath and prayed; and the night passed without further mishaps.

Unfortunately there's not a lot you can do for stomach viruses. There's no medicine that will make you feel better, and even if there were, you couldn't keep it down. The only thing you have is the infamous Pedialyte, that stuff that has saved millions of lives by keeping sick kids hydrated. Personally, I think some scientist, who must also have been a parent, created it as a dare. "Honey, if you're really sick you'll drink this. Otherwise, you're going to school." Any kid who's not on death's door will choose school over Pedialyte any day. Have you ever tasted the stuff? It's like Kool-Aid with salt and something else that I haven't identified yet and that I'd rather not know about.

Pedialyte, though intended to rehydrate kids who have been losing fluids to rather gross bodily functions, actually has the opposite effect on otherwise healthy kids. So here's my parenting tip for you this week: never confuse a Pedialyte popsicle with a jumbo Mr. Freezie. Trust me on this one. It's a very bad idea. I once gave a "Pediapop," as they're called, to Rebecca. She promptly started retching. You'd think with the great demand for this product they could invest some dollars into trying to get it to taste better. But then, I suppose, you wouldn't be able to use it as a dare any more.

As bad as it is to have your kids sick, though, there's little worse than being sick yourself and having to take care of them. You lie on the couch, praying to die, while your toddlers jump on you and every so often beg for food. You try, in an ever-so-sweet voice, to explain to your two-year-old how to get her own cereal. It doesn't work.

But getting up off the couch to fix them food is nothing compared to actually having to look at food. In fact, I think they should have a whole aisle in the supermarket dedicated to sick people. They could call it the "Norwalk Aisle." In it, you could find apple juice, applesauce, those little Premium Plus crackers, and Jell-O. And that's it. Nothing else. Because when you feel sick, the sight of ravioli or baked beans is enough to drive you over the edge.

I'm still praying that we avoid the flu this year. My husband (a doctor) has had all his shots, and he washes his hands so many times each day they're peeling (I figure he makes up for the rest of us). But if the kids do get sick, it will be nice to cuddle again. I'll just make sure they're turned the other way.

*After writing this, Katie did indeed get the flu. We did give her Pedialyte. She did think it was disgusting. We did cuddle at night, but no major mishaps occurred.*

## Warning Us to Death
*This column was first published April 7, 2003*

*I* 've been reading several news stories lately that have me pondering one question: are we really that stupid? This pops up every time I hear about a recent lawsuit against McDonald's that was, thankfully, thrown out of court. In it, several teenagers attempted to sue McDonald's because it made them fat. Here's their reasoning: McDonald's never told us that if we ate SuperSize meals five times a day it would turn us into a pile of lard, so therefore they should be held responsible and pay us millions of dollars. In other words, their case is built on the fact that not only are they fat, they are also unbelievably stupid.

It's actually not the teenagers themselves who worry me in this case, though, but the parents. What kind of parents feed their kids nothing but McDonald's? Not only that, but they also decided to parade their kids before the national media to show how large they had become. That is callous, greedy, and too many other mean words I can't print here. But it all boils down to this: we are too stupid to be expected to do the right thing, so companies have to warn us.

**We are too stupid to be expected to do the right thing, so companies have to warn us.**

And warn us they do. Buy a stroller, and chances are it comes with the warning: "Remove baby before folding." Have you ever wondered why? Because somebody, sometime, folded it with the baby inside and tried to sue them. Why do all plastic bags, medicines, turpentine, and bleach say "keep out of reach of children"? Because somebody, sometime, left these lying around with disastrous and tragic consequences.

Before companies release any product now, they have to think about all the possible ways it could be misused. I can just picture a bunch of business people, sitting around a board table, with a bunch of rubber duckies. "Okay, people, what could someone do with this ducky that could harm a child?" Silence, as they try to think inside the minds of stupid people everywhere. "They could bite its beak off and choke on it," someone may offer. From then on, all duckies will come with the warning: "Not for internal use."

Chances are it also says something like "Not to be used as a floatation device." Practically everything says "Not to be used as a floatation device," including, it seems to me, many actual floatation devices, out of fear that you may stick some water wings on a child, throw him in the deep end, and go have a nap.

There's no doubt that companies have made huge strides to promote the safety of children, with everything from car seats and child-resistant medicine caps to flame-retardant sleepwear. Much of this has only come because consumers demanded it. But what have we become if we, as parents, act as if these companies now need to take ultimate responsibility for our kids?

Parents were once considered to have little excuse if their children came to harm. Part of being a parent was to provide a protective hedge around them. Today, an alien visiting our planet would assume parents can't be trusted with anything.

Tragically, too many parents live up to this reputation, disregarding these warnings, and hurting kids in the process. But I can't help but wonder if all these warnings, instead of making such harm remote, actually, in some way, increase its likelihood. We are teaching people to not think for themselves, that they cannot be expected to make the right choices. But there are just too many things that can harm kids, and we'll never be able to put warnings on everything. Parents are the last wall of defence between our kids and harm. We have to accept this responsibility ourselves and be vigilant, rather than expecting others to be vigilant for us.

What would society be like if we expected parents to be responsible like this? We might hold people to certain standards of parenting. Instead, when I go grocery shopping later today, my cart will say "Do not leave child unattended." If we need to be told that, then we truly have a parenting crisis. I don't think things are nearly that bad. But with each new lawsuit and new warning, I sometimes have to wonder.

*I originally wrote this column a little differently. I had the company executives trying to figure out what one could possibly do wrong with that rubber ducky, when one pipes up, "They could stick it up their bum!" at which point they affix the warning "Not for internal use." Young children, as any parent knows, have an odd obsession with toilet habits and farting. I had young children at the time, so I thought this was very funny. When one is farther away from that stage of life, though, such talk may have other connotations. Everyone I tested my first version on thought of these connotations, too. So I changed it. I still think the original is funnier, but there you go.*

## Why Aren't We Dead?
*This column was first published January 5, 2004*

A s I look at my daughters and contemplate the arrival of the new year, I can't help but think, I'm glad we're not dead!

It's actually quite surprising. Think of all those things you did as a child that you would never, in a million years, allow your child to do. Our own parents and grandparents, for instance, weren't aware of the need to bleach countertops to prevent infection, and so spent blissful lives thinking about such mundane things as "I hope that fireplace doesn't burn our all-wood house down." They had petty concerns compared to the lists of things we must be constantly vigilant about.

The holidays have just passed, which reminds me of a "new" danger. We use stuffing to actually stuff a turkey. Think of all those potential germs! According to the powers that be at Health Canada, we are supposed to cook the stuffing in a separate container and hope that, just by being in the same oven as the bird, the stuffing will acquire taste through osmosis. By the time our kids are adults, they will consider us cave people for trying to make our food tasty.

Until that time, though, we can sit in judgment over our own Stone-Age parents. Our mothers, for instance, when doing up our coats, used to tie up our hoods, despite the obvious risk of strangulation. Our parents painted our houses with lead paint. They installed inefficient furnaces but didn't bother to invent carbon monoxide monitors. They took us swimming at local beaches, thinking they were "building memories" but ignoring that "building bacteria count" from the raw waste that companies dumped in the water. And they didn't always supervise us.

When my father-in-law was younger, his mother would pack him a lunch, pour him a thermos full of hot chocolate, and watch him head out to a nearby lake to play hockey all day with the neighbourhood boys. Even the youngest would be gone for upwards of eight hours, without adults to prevent bodychecking, investigate the thickness of the ice, or watch for suspicious strangers. Of course, any pervert that propositioned a stick-wielding boy who could play hockey all day in sub-zero temperatures probably would have had a death wish, but we modern-day parents would still never dream of leaving our youngsters alone.

But forget about protecting our innocence; what about our heads? Those boys on the ice had no helmets. Come to think of it, my generation didn't even wear bicycle helmets. We did wear seat belts, though our own parents didn't. People drove after they were drinking—even while they were drinking! And when your parents brought you home from the hospital, chances are they put you on your mother's lap. No car seat for you! It's a miracle that we lived long enough to even become parents.

When we were children, we weren't afraid to eat peanut butter (now there's one safety hazard that is demonstrably getting worse). We slept on our stomachs when we were babies, because our mothers hadn't heard of SIDS. We had no antibacterial soap. Yet all the energy that goes into all the new safety measures, let alone the emotional energy that is spent every time we hear a new health warning, is disproportionate to the risks. Today's children are safer than any other generation in history, but you wouldn't necessarily know that by reading all the "news bulletins" in the parenting magazines. This isn't to say bad things can't happen, only that it's far less likely that they will.

As parents it's easy to become obsessed with all the things that can possibly hurt our kids. These concerns, though, are largely luxuries. We can only worry about preservatives once we have surplus food to preserve. We can only worry about strings around hoods, which have caused 17 deaths in the United States since 1985, when vaccines have virtually eliminated measles, a disease that until relatively recently killed over 500 children a year. That's not to say we shouldn't try to keep our kids safe. But let's relax a little. If current trends continue, chances are we'll live to see many, many more new years. Even if I do keep stuffing my turkey.

## My Big, Fat Baby
*This column was first published July 28, 2003*

My youngest daughter turned six yesterday. I think I should have been the one getting the presents.

Having Katie pretty near killed me. Five days before Katie was born I called my husband at work, called my mother at work, and told them both to get home because the baby was coming. Mom arrived to look after Rebecca, and Keith and I went to the hospital, where they pronounced me not in labour.

Two nights later, at 2:00 a.m., I woke up my husband, called my mother, and ventured to the hospital again, certain that this time was it. They told me it wasn't.

The next night it happened again. Katie was my third baby. It's not like I didn't know what contractions felt like. These felt like contractions. I hadn't slept for a week. And worst of all, people were starting to get mad at me. When I called my mother at midnight two nights later, she almost wouldn't come. She was exhausted, and she had a meeting first thing in the morning. My husband told me that I'd better be sure this time.

Luckily, as soon as we arrived they said the baby was coming, hooked me up to the IV, and told me to relax. Within a few minutes, though, I had the nurse back in the room. "The epidural's not working," I said. "I feel pain. I'm not supposed to feel pain!"

> When I called my mother at midnight two nights later, she almost wouldn't come.

"Oh, the epidural just hasn't kicked in," she replied nonchalantly, walking out of the room.

I started reciting. That breathing thing never really worked for me. It didn't distract me enough. So when Rebecca was born, I tried reciting "The Lord Is My Shepherd" instead. It required concentration, but I knew it well enough that I could pull it off. "The Lord Is my Shepherd" helped me through Rebecca, and it helped me through Christopher. But this was different. This was PAIN.

"The Lord is my shepherd, I shall not—get that nurse back in here, NOW!—want, He makes me lie down—why are you still standing there? NOW!—in green pastures..."

By the time the doctor arrived I was starting to forget the words. "He makes me lie down—(WHACK! WHACK! on Keith's stomach) WHERE? Where does He make me LIE DOWN?"

Keith said, "In green pastures, honey, in green pastures."

"In green pastures. He leadeth me—WHERE?" (WHACK! WHACK!)

"Oomph. Beside still waters. And honey, you have tension in your jaw. Remember? Don't clench your teeth, honey. We want loose, not tension."

WHACK! WHACK! "FINE. The Lord is my Shepherd. I shall NOT (WHACK!) CLENCH (WHACK!) MY TEETH (WHACK! WHACK!)."

The nurse later commented that in all her years in the delivery room, she had heard the Lord's name used in many creative ways, but never quite like that.

Katie came along pretty soon after that. She was 9 pounds (and I'm pretty tiny). I have never quite forgiven her. She was also really ugly. She was all purple and wrinkled and looked odd. I can say that, of course, because she is absolutely gorgeous now. If she were still ugly, I'd never admit I thought so then.

Unfortunately, my mother failed to load the film in our camera correctly (something that all but cancels out the lack of sleep I gave her that week), so we don't have any pictures of her first few days. By the time the pictures turned out, she was no longer as ugly. So you'll just have to take my word for it.

I can look back on the whole thing and laugh now. You really do forget the pain. During my pregnancy with Katie, I threw up prolifically, I had constant searing pain in my legs, and I had contractions for the last two months. She also gave me varicose veins I had to eventually have removed (now there's a gross surgery). And when I look at her today, I know I'd do it again in a minute. So maybe I don't need a present. Maybe all I need to do is watch her as she plays and sings, and kiss her tonight as she sleeps. She'll always be my big, fat, ugly baby that I love more than I can imagine. Happy birthday, honey.

*Katie thinks this story is hilarious. She's always going around announcing, "I was a big, fat baby!" puffing her cheeks out and stomping around like a giant. It's very cute.*

## I'm Glad I'm Grown Up
*This column was first published July 19, 2004*

We often say to our kids, "These are the best years of your life." We remember with fondness the days when we could ride our bikes, skip stones, watch TV, and play with friends, all without having to worry about paying bills.

But think about how your kid interprets that life. He doesn't get to choose his classmates. He has to sit beside Billy, who makes fun of his glasses, picks on him at recess, tries to take his cookies at lunch, and copies off of his test papers. He has to get on the bus with Janice, who sits beside him and still sends him Valentine's Day cards in March, causing all the other boys to laugh at him for having a "girlfriend."

And worst of all, he doesn't get to decide what to eat. If he wants a cookie, you tell him it's too close to dinner. If he wants one after dinner, you tell him he can't have one because he didn't eat his dinner. If he informs you that the reason he didn't eat his dinner was because it tasted like puke, you send him to his room. The quest for that cookie takes more emotional energy than many of us adults spend trying to figure out how we're going to pay the credit card bill.

We may look back on childhood and think it was blissful. But in reality, if we really stopped to think about it, we'd take adulthood any time.

Most of us no longer have to hang out with the likes of Billy. If there's a bully at work, we can usually avoid him or her. He can make absolutely no difference to our lives any more, because we can largely dictate where we go and whom we go with.

We can decide what to watch on TV, how late we're going to stay up, how much money we get to spend on hobbies, where we live, and what we wear.

We can stash chocolate up on a shelf where the kids won't see it, and we don't have to share it (I speak from experience). That Russell Stover box of chocolate truffles can go an awfully long way, because there's no mother standing over our shoulders saying, "Now make sure you give your friends one, too, so that it's fair." There's no such thing as fair. The way I see it, as an adult, if I buy it, it's mine, as long as I can find a good enough hiding place.

If I don't like my job, I can leave. This may be scary, and it may require retraining, but I have some control over it. A kid can't decide not to go to school.

If I don't like my clothes, I can get new ones. I don't have to wear that sweater Grandma knit me that scratches.

If I want to read a book that my brothers or sisters

think is stupid, I can do so in peace. I can do so in a bubble bath, even at 3 in the morning.

If I have friends over, no one's reminding me that I better share everything I hold dear. My friends don't immediately go into my bedroom and start ruffling through my underwear drawer or my closets to see what "good stuff" I might have in there. They don't take all my precious things off the shelves and pile them onto the floor for me to clean up once they're gone. They don't whisper, "Do you have anything good in the fridge?"

As long as I remember to take off my makeup every night, I'm rarely greeted in the morning by a huge zit that threatens to render me a social pariah for the rest of my life.

Boys no longer snap my bra straps.

Kids may not have to worry about the things that typically give adults pause, but they still have to negotiate their share of land mines. Instead of our lectures, then, maybe what they really need is some compassion and support. Personally, I'd take my bubble bath, my hidden chocolates, my silly novels, and my own choice of clothes over their lives any time. I like being a grown-up. It's hard to be a kid. I'm proud of my kids for doing it so well.

# Parenting Traps

In parenting, as in life, we have to keep an eye out for the danger signs. It's easy for little behavioural problems or bad attitudes to fester and begin to make your life—and that of your family—miserable. Often as parents we reinforce negative behaviour without realizing it, because it's easier than dealing with the problem. Here are a number of columns I wrote to be the "Warning" signs for us travelling along this parenting road.

## Avoiding the Self-Esteem Trap

*This column was first published August 26, 2002*

I have a confession to make. My daughters (ages 5 and 8) are not actually enrolled in soccer this summer. I'm not sure if this is illegal or not—Matthew Perry of "Friends" once said that it was illegal for young boys not to play hockey in Canada—but if it is, I hope that society will go easy on me. The truth is, my kids have been involved in so many after-school activities this year that we're looking forward to a bit of a break.

But most of my friends have signed up their kids for soccer, and I understand why. Kids love it; it's not nearly as competitive as hockey; and nobody looks like an idiot. The little girls wandering off to pick wild-flowers still look like stars when they realize the ball is coming and they jump into the fray, dandelion necklaces and all!

Best of all, though, is the uninterrupted time we can spend cheering our kids on. Kids simply crave our attention. All of us have, at some time or another, been inundated by constant "Mom, look at me" or "Dad, watch this!" as we try to have a conversation. Kids won't feel like they are successful until you as a parent tell them they are. That's why kids who have lost a parent through desertion often have a hard time sorting out their identities. They feel unaffirmed.

**Kids won't feel like they are successful until you as a parent tell them they are.**

Nevertheless, I think we can take this quest for self-esteem too far. I once read a study from the February 1996 *Psychological Review* that said that the majority of American inmates on death row had very high self-esteem—and that *that* may be part of the problem!

Perhaps our difficulty in understanding whether high self-esteem or low self-esteem is to blame for society's problems is that we don't know what self-esteem is. Essentially, it means to feel good about ourselves. But all of us know someone—maybe at work, or on our street, or in our own families—who feels just great about himself or herself but who everyone else firmly believes is a complete jerk. Some things aren't worth feeling good about.

I remember one time I just lost it with my daughters. The house was a mess; I was trying to get dinner ready; and I had asked them repeatedly to clean up. Instead they were just dawdling. Finally I started yelling hysterically, and soon we all ended up in tears. Did I have high self-esteem then? No, I felt like a pretty bad mother. And maybe that was a good thing, because I knew I had problems both with anger and with finding strategies to get them to obey me, and I needed to work on both. In short, I had an accurate picture of myself.

And in the end that's what we should strive for. I want my daughters to know what they're good at, what they're not good at, and where they need to improve. I want them to have standards. I don't want them to feel they're the best at everything, which is often what we tell them. Let's say a four-year-old boy draws a picture he knows he didn't try very hard at, and you gush all over it and say how great it is. Or your ten-year-old daughter shows you a report she's thrown together in under ten minutes, and you proclaim it wonderful. They know they didn't work at these things. They know they're garbage. So they learn that you have no taste and not to trust what you say.

But if you say something like "That's an interesting picture, Timmy, but I've seen you draw better ones," or, "Well, Julie, what do you think of the report?" you challenge them to analyze themselves accurately. And that's what counts.

So as I think of parents out on the soccer fields, I'm glad they're there cheering their children on, whether or not they're successful, as long as they try. But maybe we should think hard before we cheer on *everything* they do. Our kids are only human. Let's help them deal with their weaknesses, revel in their successes, and see life through clear glasses.

## Screaming in Wal-Mart
*This column was first published January 6, 2003*

A few weeks ago my husband, a pediatrician, overheard a two-minute "inspirational moment" telling parents how to deal with temper tantrums, after which he felt like throwing one himself. The "expert's" advice went something like this: children, the poor darlings, need to be encouraged to share their precious feelings, so you should hug a child in the midst of a tantrum (even if she persists in punching and kicking) to encourage her to tell you why she's angry.

Yet do toddlers even understand their feelings? Many are new to them, so when they feel something intensely, they get scared and lash out. Besides, is our goal really to bring up children who will express *all* their feelings? "Well, Mommy, I really feel like biting and kicking Jimmy right now because he has a nicer train than me, so I think I will."

Of course not! When we're angry, we don't just punch people—at least I hope we don't—we try to calm ourselves down. It's the same with kids. They don't need to be encouraged to express their feelings; instead, they need to be taught how to manage them appropriately. And that's something, in the end, that only they can do. If we are the ones always calming them down (by giving them candy or distracting them or just hugging them), they'll never learn to do it themselves. While distraction works well for infants, by the time they're older they're capable of learning to calm themselves down, to everybody's benefit.

That sounds very straightforward, but I know it's completely useless when your kid is screaming in Wal-Mart because he wants to sit in the cart but there's no room now that you've added the family-sized toilet paper. And meanwhile every other shopper is looking at you like you're the parental equivalent of pond scum.

So what do you do? You ditch the toilet paper, stick the kid in the cart, and buy some candy to shut that precious darling up so no one else will see that pond-scum resemblance. And in the process, you've guaranteed that every time you go shopping from now on, your kid will throw more fits so that he will be chauffeured and stuffed with goodies.

I have spent many time outs in the Wal-Mart parking lot with the radio on while a child screamed in the back seat. Every now and then, I'd say firmly, "Rebecca, we are not leaving until we finish shopping. But we aren't doing that until you stop crying, so you are wasting your own playtime." And then I continued to sing along with Shania while I tried not to fume. For a brief time Rebecca, and to a lesser extent Katie, were regulars in this time-out parking lot, or time-out bedroom, or even time-out sidewalk outside a restaurant. Thankfully they soon learned that it wasn't worth their while.

Kids need limits. They don't need coddling. It's not trendy to think that these days, but it's true. Obedience was once considered a virtue in childhood. Today, *obey* is considered a four-letter word. We wouldn't want to try and control our little darlings and harm their creativity, would we?

Giving kids limits, though, actually *helps* their creativity. If we coddle kids when they misbehave, they learn they have absolute power. That much control is scary to a kid. They run around like a little pinball machine, trying to fly up against a wall and find a limit. Instead of exploring creatively, they focus on finding their safety net.

It's hard not to give in to a screaming child in public. But we harm our kids if we don't help them to learn self-control. The rest of us observers, though, can help parents teach these kinds of lessons. Instead of looking judgmental next time we see a child screaming in public, perhaps we should think about helping that parent out. We could say, "Don't worry; every child does this. Just stand firm," to let the mother know she's not alone. Parent or not, we can all play a part in creating a Wal-Mart—and a society—that is tantrum free. Now that's a desire worth expressing.

## Cries in the Night

*This column was first published March 10, 2003*

know you mothers may find this hard to imagine, but I swear it's true. A few nights ago, Katie woke up crying. *And Keith woke up before I did.* I know, I know, it seems unbelievable. But he actually took care of the whole thing, and I only woke up briefly to wonder what he was doing out of bed.

My husband's wonderful. But when it comes to

nighttime demands from children, I've generally found that he is, like most husbands, more or less useless.

This starts, I think, because men can't nurse the baby. And when that baby is subsequently weaned, the husband isn't used to responding to cries in the night, so the wife keeps getting up anyway.

If his pager goes off, though, Keith is up like a rocket. He can prescribe drugs when thirty seconds ago he was in la-la land. But if our girls cry, he usually doesn't hear it. Once, when we lived in Toronto, I was getting really sick of this. Rebecca was crying; Keith was snoring; and I was ready to scream. So I paged him. He woke up, called in for messages, and was told he needed to go get the baby. I haven't resorted to the method since, and now I may not ever need to, since he's getting up with the kids, too.

I don't think, though, that this is because he's suddenly become more attuned to their every need. I think it's because I've become less attuned. Now that our girls generally sleep through the night, can make it to the toilet if they need to puke, and don't pee in their beds, there's less need for me to be on full alert at two in the morning. But it was not always that way.

Our kids were not great sleepers. My mother-in-law claims that her kids slept through the night when they were a month old. Obviously that trait skips a generation, because we never experienced it. And when Rebecca hit six months old, I was desperate.

A lot of parents go through this, but the solutions we pick can often make the problem worse. The most common is to let the kid sleep with you, something many experts advise. In the Middle Ages, the theory goes, everyone slept together, so why don't we do it now? Well, in the Middle Ages, if you went to a hotel you also slept in the same bed as several assorted strangers, as well as numerous fleas and bedbugs. That may have been perfectly natural back then, but trust me, if the Quality Inn started pulling that stunt they'd lose a lot of business.

Nevertheless, sleeping all together is seen as a great solution. The kid is less likely to wake up, and at least you don't need to get out of bed when they do. But here's the thing: my kids are not quiet sleepers. They flail, they groan, and they snort. And when they were babies, they also made those little sucking sounds, which are ever so cute when you're leaning over the crib and ever so annoying when you're trying to drift off.

And then there's the other problem: kids grow. And once they grow, they kick. Hard. Trust me. Every now and then Katie still climbs into bed, and then, when I'm in the middle of a wonderful dream, OOMPH. Right in the stomach. Or else she punches me in the eye.

Then there's the perennial problem of romance. Some kids may not start off in your bed but do come in during the night, often at not-so-opportune times, if you get my drift. So there you and your spouse are, attempting to get "reacquainted," when who should decide to jump between you but your adorable toddler who wants to snuggle, too.

I never realized how important sleep was until I had kids and I no longer slept. If you're exhausted and desperate, I know how you feel. Next week, I'll tell you some of what doctors recommend. And then I'll tell you what I'd really advise you to do.

# Sleep Like a Baby

*This column was first published March 17, 2003*

*I*f somebody came into your bedroom in the middle of the night and flicked on the light and stole your pillow, would you be able to get back to sleep? Probably not, with all the commotion of calling the police and searching for intruders, but that's not the point I'm trying to make right now. No, most of us wouldn't be able to sleep, because our "sleep cues" would be gone. Babies are exactly the same. They need certain conditions to sleep, too, conditions that we teach them, even if we don't realize it. These are the conditions that we taught our youngest daughter, Katie:

First, Katie needed to be nursed to sleep while being rocked in a rocking chair. Then, when it looked like she was in a deep sleep, she had to be lifted without any change in the angle of her body, even if this required the parent (in this case, the one with mammary glands) to throw her own back out as she rose from the chair. Then, said mother had to frantically call "Keith, Keith, get in here!" in order to summon the other parent (the one without mammary glands) to rearrange the blankets and lower the crib rail (since the mother forgot to do this before she started nursing). Everything thus readied, the mother would attempt the perfect transfer without changing the angle of the baby's body.

If any of these conditions were not met—and, in many cases, even if they were—this baby would cry. In this case, what this baby needed was to be transferred to the swing. Once she was again in a deep sleep, you could pick her up and transfer her to the crib (once again whispering frantically for the other parent to get the blankets ready). This was a much more dangerous transfer, because it necessitated changing the angle of the baby's body, which usually woke her up, sending you back to step one (nurse her in a rocking chair). Because this was our nightly ritual—and our middle-of-the-night ritual—Katie could get to sleep no other way.

One day we smartened up. We read a book (*Solve your Child's Sleep Problems* by Richard Ferber) that said that babies need to be taught how to go to sleep by themselves. They need to be put in their crib while still awake, both at set nap times and set bedtimes, so that they get used to putting themselves to sleep. Otherwise, you're teaching your baby to need you to fall asleep, and whenever they wake in the middle of the night they'll call for you again. Reading this was like that revelation at the end of *Planet of the Apes*, when the main character surveys the desolation and collapses in grief and despair as he realizes, "We did this to ourselves!"

With a renewed sense of resolve, we embraced this marvellous new plan. In principle. Until we tried it. If we thought we had heard screaming before, it was nothing compared to what we heard afterwards.

But we weren't as heartless as it may sound. Part of this plan is returning to the child's room every few minutes, to reassure your baby that you still love him or her. Then you must leave again. In our case, this was usually accomplished by my husband carrying me from the room as he hissed, "You promised we would go by the book for a week," and I struggled to get back to my baby.

Thus banished from her room, I would rock back and forth on my bed, like characters in a movie who have been in solitary confinement and have gone stark raving mad, as I listened to my baby cry. I had earplugs in my ears, and I would stare at my clock, mumbling, "I can go in again in three minutes and twenty seconds, in three minutes and nineteen seconds…"

But the amazing thing was, Katie learned to sleep. She only cried for twenty minutes that first night, and only a few minutes the next few nights after that. And she started taking naps, too, once we made them at regular times. And once she started to sleep, she started to smile. So did I. And we haven't stopped.

## Anger Is Not Like Flatulence
*This column was first published November 17, 2003*

We have a problem at the dinner table. One of our adorable, angelic daughters has a habit of emitting flatulent gas audibly during meals. In other words, she farts. Loudly. Loudly enough to cause her and her sister to convulse into fits of laughter, which usually results in more gas being emitted and at least one daughter falling out of her chair.

We have tried to explain to this daughter that silent-but-deadly farts are actually more polite than loud ones, but to no avail. When you've got to get it out, she says, you've got to get it out.

While we were busy confronting this problem, I overheard a radio program on a similar theme. Anger, most people believe, needs to be released or it, too, will bubble up inside you until you explode. And once you release it, supposedly you will feel better. In other words, anger must be like farting. But I don't believe anger works that way. When we're angry, if we let it out all at once, we may not get rid of it. In fact, venting anger can actually make us angrier, unless we do it carefully. When we're angry, we often use harsher words than we really mean. And "reckless words pierce like a sword." Those words can hurt the other person horribly, making them angry, too.

My kids get along wonderfully 95% of the time. But when they get angry, the house is filled with wails of "You never want to play with me!" or "You're such a mean sister!" until finally you hear "I don't want to play with you ever again!" and a door slams somewhere. When such words are said, both girls invariably end up in indignant tears.

Thankfully, though, our house is now becoming more peaceful, thanks to an object lesson I have recently tried. Here's what you do: take two paper plates, two tubes of toothpaste, two popsicle sticks, and a $10 bill. Tell the kids to empty their tubes of toothpaste onto the paper plates, and then tell them whoever gets the toothpaste back in the tube first can have the $10. Don't worry; you won't be out any money. The task simply can't be done. Toothpaste, like words, can't be put back in. Once it's out, it's out.

We adults need this lesson, too. After all, if our relationships with our family members are the most precious things to us, then we should make sure we're treating them with tender care. Running a steamroller over our beloveds as we list all their real and imaginary faults isn't exactly protecting those relationships.

We've had to learn this the hard way, since my husband and I are both very stubborn and hotheaded. It's one reason I've never spanked my kids; I'm afraid if I let myself, I'd do it in anger. Instead, when I'm really mad, I usually tell the kids to go anywhere, as long as they're not near me, until I have a chance to calm down and sort out an appropriate response. This usually makes them very penitent, as they both hate having to be alone, and so defuses the situation for all of us.

Sometimes everyone needs a time out. Perhaps you need to put that colicky baby into a playpen and take some deep breaths, or to tell that wayward teenager who walked in at 2:30 in the morning that you'll discuss it tomorrow when you've all had a chance to calm down. Or maybe, when your husband arrives home late from work again, it's time to go for coffee with a girlfriend to give your white-hot wrath a chance to simmer down so you can discuss the issue later constructively.

The last time my kids had a fight I explained this concept to them. Anger is not like farting. You can't just blow up at each other; you need to identify the real problem and talk about only that. I don't know if they completely understand, but they've really caught on to the slogan. Let's all treat our most precious relationships with the care they deserve. Maybe there are things that need changing, but don't just attack someone you love. You can never put that toothpaste back in the tube.

*My kids loved this column. Wherever we went for the next week or so, somebody would invariably size up the girls and ask, "Now which one of you is it?" causing them both to laugh again and—well, you can guess it. I still won't reveal which one it is, but suffice it to say that they enjoyed the attention.*

*Many also told me they appreciated the message.*
*I spoke with one mom whose relationship had*
*broken up, and she was trying to keep her child*
*completely out of the conflicts between her and*
*her ex. The ex, though, got angry and would fre-*
*quently involve the child in his problems. "You*
*can't put that toothpaste back in the tube." She*
*wished he understood that, and I hope many*
*more of us will remember that lesson.*

## The Gifts We Should be Celebrating
*This column was first published March 1, 2004*

*I*n a letter to the editor, a reader pointed out
that in a recent column on the school system I
had omitted what was perhaps the most important ele-
ment in a successful educational experience: the
teacher. He's absolutely right. Teachers can take the
worst class and turn it around, inspiring kids towards
lifelong learning. But here's the catch: we can't rely on
truly great teachers to change the educational land-
scape, because there just aren't that many of them. For
the record, I don't think he was implying there were; it's
just an interesting argument, so I'd like to pursue it a
little further.

When I reflect on my own schooling experience, I
can recall four truly great teachers. Luckily, I only had
three truly awful ones. I would say the ratio was
roughly 4 great, 23 fine, 3 awful. As we were driving to
the garage to retrieve our ailing vehicle (we had to call
CAA again!), I asked Keith what he thought. He was

more optimistic—6 great, 23 fine, 1 awful—but then, he was educated in Belleville.

Most teachers are indeed good, competent, and fun. They're just not great. Great teaching is a gift; you can't learn it in teachers' college. When it comes to educational policy, though, people often zero in on some particularly gifted teacher who transformed 25 inner-city illiterate gang leaders into national chess champions in a year, and try to reform the system based on what she did. These stories are heartwarming, and I subscribe to *Reader's Digest* just for the monthly communion with the Kleenex box they afford me. But we can't copy what these teachers are doing, because it's not a formula. It's a person. And they can't be everywhere at once, so they can't change our system.

This line of reasoning started me thinking about encouraging our children in their gifts. I think we're all gifted in some particular way, whether it's in physical skills, mental skills, or social skills. As a parent, it's important to find out what your own child's unique gifts are and then to nurture them. That's not always easy, because sometimes the things they're gifted in aren't things we particularly value or know much about. One of my daughters is an amazing artist. I find this odd, since my last successful painting experience was turning one wall green without splattering on the baseboards, something for which my husband was extremely grateful and rather surprised. Art, though, is easy to value. Sometimes our children are gifted in ways that we don't like. A bookworm parent gives birth to a jock and works hard to steer his interests in another direction. It's wonderful to stretch our children, but let's not deny who they are.

Other times the obstacles aren't with us parents but with our kids' culture. It's awfully hard being a kid. We look at our children and think, "You have it so easy! You have nothing you need to worry about!" But they do worry. They live in a nerve-racking social environment that only values certain personalities. If children are being teased at school, they can't leave. For us the story is different. If there's somebody we don't like at work, we can always get another job. Children are trapped. Many children, like those who love books or quiet kids with lots of empathy, actually have to work to try to suppress these natural giftings to fit in.

Friends of ours have a very bright son who has always done well in school. This year he's become moody and belligerent because he's been clashing with his teacher. He's always challenging her, asking "why." That's a great trait for a future scientist, but it doesn't help you in elementary school. Likewise, a child who can't concentrate in school because he needs constant stimulation may make one of the world's best stockbrokers in the future. He just can't function now.

Our kids may not fit the mould, but that doesn't mean they aren't gifted at something. Childhood is an artificial environment. If we can help our kids find the ways that they are gifted, even if it's in a way schools don't necessarily recognize, we give them hope for the future. And when everybody finds their gifts and uses them, just like those truly great teachers have done, everybody wins.

*Interestingly, one of the teachers I would call truly great now, in retrospect, I certainly didn't like then. She was my grade-nine-history teacher. I don't remember a thing about what we learned in history, but boy did we learn how to write essays. She made us write introductory paragraphs again and again and again until we got our thesis statement right. She helped me to write more than any English teacher I ever had, and I'm grateful to her, despite the hard time I gave her back then.*

## Your Child's Expert

*This column was first published February 23, 2004*

*I* spent a week last summer reminding myself why I hated being a teenager. I was working as office manager at a camp while my kids were campers. They could see me at mealtimes, so they didn't get too homesick, but on the whole they were on their own. In the meantime, I listened to counsellors fretting about boyfriends or girlfriends, about conflicts between friends, and about who is in what clique.

That's not all I heard. Just like me, a nurse also came up to work while her three kids attended camp, including one very shy 8-year-old boy. She was supposed to be working at his camp, but was sent instead to the one for teenagers, on the other side of the lake. Her son didn't fare very well in her absence. The 19-year-old section head and 18-year-old counsellor were sure they knew why. "In our experience," they said, "these kids do much better if the parents are completely off-site."

Now these teenagers were lovely people and experienced campers, having spent 8 weeks at camp for the last three years. But she was an expert, too. She could have said, "I know you've spent 168 days at camp, but I have 3,000 days of experience with this particular boy, and he would have been fine had I worked here." It was not to be. She took their criticism lying down.

This incident stayed with me, I think, because it's not an anomaly. Everywhere we turn, someone else is telling us how to raise our kids (including me!). Even the spanking debate, which I sparked again a few weeks ago (why do I do these things?), is symptomatic of this need for others to tell us—despite divided research data—how to parent our children.

One of my friends recently had an unfortunate run-in with a teacher, who was upset that this mom helped her fourth grade daughter to understand math. "She has to learn it the way we teach it, not the way you explain it," the teacher stressed, failing to see the irony that if the teacher had actually taught the child, she wouldn't have needed her mother's help in the first place. The mother said little. I think a simple "my child, my house, my time" would have sufficed, followed by, in a Shrek accent, "Bye-bye. See you later." But my friend was more polite.

Instead of feeling upset when someone criticizes what we do with our kids, we tend to feel intimidated. When Rebecca took swimming lessons at the age of 4, the swimming instructor dunked her. I knew this wouldn't work, but I didn't speak up, and to this day I wonder why I was so cowed by a 17-year-old. It took me two years to undo the damage, during which my daughter would scream if I mentioned lessons. I took her swimming for fun, and she slowly began to like the water again. She swims like a fish now! Yet she wasn't like most kids when it comes to learning to swim. She's easily spooked, and I should have stepped in earlier.

We live in an expert-driven society. No longer does common sense or life experience qualify you for anything. Yet, though experts may know general knowledge, such as what happens with most children, you are the only one who knows the specifics or what happens with your child.

I say this knowing what it is like to be on the other side. My husband, a pediatrician, often deals with parents who refuse to believe that nothing is wrong with their child. We could all benefit from two or three honest and wise friends who could act as our personal "reality checks," telling us when we, or our kids, are out of line. But I still can't help feeling that erring on the side of too much involvement is better than erring on the side of too little. Studies show consistently that kids need involved parents. Good teachers and principals know this and welcome it; insecure ones don't.

Maybe you don't have much education. Maybe you haven't read all the parenting books, and maybe you've even made mistakes. But your child will likely never have a better advocate than you. Next time somebody starts telling me that I should leave my children alone or butt out, I will leave. But my children come with me. Bye-bye. See you later.

## Image Isn't Everything
*This column was first published April 19, 2004*

K ids like heroes. Today, though, *hero* seems to be synonymous with *famous*, and many who are famous did little of merit to get that way. Yet fame has opened doors. Entertain the president in private, and you're given your own line of purses. Arrange to break the knees of your main competition in the Olympics, and you're invited on reality-TV shows. Fame is its own currency.

Earlier this year, when he was running for the Democratic nomination in the States, Howard Dean received a standing ovation for his endorsement by Martin Sheen, whose only real claim to fame is that he plays a president on TV. It reminded me of a 9/11 TV benefit I watched, where actors Jimmy Smits and Dennis Franz said, "We're not policemen, but we play ones on TV," as if that gave them credibility to talk about those who had really risked—and lost—their lives.

> **I find it very odd that we give so much credence to celebrities.**

I find it very odd that we give so much credence to celebrities. I remember a *Good Housekeeping* cover article promising to share "Julia Roberts' Lessons on Love." Now I love Julia Roberts' movies. But why in the world would I want love advice from a woman who left two men at the altar, divorced another, and finally stole one from another woman so she could marry him? I'd rather hear love advice from a couple who has been married fifty years, endured financial problems and grief, and still are all over each other. Yet Julia's hardly the worst offender. Her kind of behaviour seems oddly normal, since at least she's aiming for domestic bliss. Many of the celebrities our kids follow don't even have that on their radar screen.

Celebrities live outside of the real, where bad choices seemingly have no consequences. Money and fame cover a multitude of problems. What really matters is how you appear. If children are in tune with pop culture—and almost all are—they're going to get a very distorted picture of life. You may have a lovely daughter who works hard in school, who befriends the special-ed child in her class, and who helps with the dishes without being asked. But this same child, whom you thank God for every day, could be almost suicidal because she isn't popular. As adults it's easy to forget how important these things are when you're 13, 14, or even 17. We know that those who were popular then are not necessarily successful today, and having a gaggle of friends at 15 is not the same as having real relationships when you're 35. But at that moment, your life is reduced to acne and the label on your jeans.

Image is not everything, but that's not the message kids hear when they watch TV, watch movies, or listen to music. They learn that happiness comes from what one looks like on the outside, rather than from relationships and accomplishments, two things that can't happen in a world where consequences are non-existent and character is not as important as popularity. As much as possible, even if it makes your brain hurt, try to tune in to what they're tuning in to. Don't yell about their music being too loud; listen to it with them. Watch their movies together, so you can talk about what you've seen and show them how real life may actually be better.

Engaging them, though, isn't the only thing we have to do. Last week I talked about how detrimental TV could be to young children whose brains are still forming. What about teens whose identities are still forming? One study recently found that one of the five best predictors of emotional health in teenagers was *not having* a phone or television in their bedrooms. Those, of course, may sound like fighting words. But you are the parent. TV, computers, and even the phone are privileges. They aren't rights. Besides, wouldn't it be better—and safer—to have your teen surf the net in the kitchen, while you read a book nearby, both of you enjoying cups of hot chocolate together?

These are vulnerable years. Don't leave your kids to the lions. Image isn't everything, but they won't know that unless we give them a real life full of real relationships, real consequences, and real love.

# Making a House a Home

One of my passions is to help parents focus on what's really important—their relationships with their kids—rather than on all the other stuff, like keeping a perfect house, being in all the right after-school activities, and generally driving yourself nuts with too many demands. My book *To Love, Honor and Vacuum: When you feel more like a maid than a mother* deals with all of these issues in greater detail.

But here's a glimpse into my attitude toward house and home: people matter more than things; you do need some order; but let's get that housework and cooking out of the way quickly so there's more time for games. Oh, and by the way, teach your kids to clean toilets. I think that's about it. You can read on now for more detail.

## Of Crumbs and Clutter

*This column was first published September 23, 2002*

Last spring I attended the large funeral of a lovely man who died far too early. The processional to his gravesite threatened to engulf all of Sidney Street, so we carpooled to make it shorter. I crawled into the van of my friend Wanda, who was eager to play chauffeur until she recalled with horror the state of her vehicle.

You see, Wanda has five children. And what that means is that Wanda's van was filled with empty (and some not-so-empty) Reid's Dairy milkshake cups, library books, homework assignments, backpacks, a pair of flippers (don't ask me why), some clothes, and lots of other things. Wanda, of course, was mortified to have us witness this. I thought this was funny, since I knew my van was in the same state and I only have two kids to blame it on!

**If we were ever stranded, we could survive for several days just on what's behind the booster seats.**

At any given moment, I have at least ten of those ridiculous toys they give out with kids' meals littering my floor, along with countless plastic wrappers from who knows what, receipts, and, above all, crumbs. I console myself by saying that if we were ever stranded in the middle of nowhere, we could survive for several days just on what's behind the booster seats.

Kids are messy, and we shouldn't pretend otherwise. I would like to affix a notice on my door that says "By entering this house, you agree to recognize that small people live here. You realize that means more mess than any human being can reasonably be expected to clean up. You will agree not to look behind any furniture or to survey the front hall with disdain or to notice if something feels squishy when you sit on the couch." Underneath this warning would be a contract they would have to sign in triplicate, so if they ever try to make fun of my house, I can remind them of their promise.

That being said, I also know that we can't just let our houses get taken over by mess. For one thing, it's just too exhausting. The Learning Annex in Toronto is even offering a course in "de-cluttering," for the simple reason that "de-cluttering" is one of the best things to do to reduce stress! Speaking as the mother of two young kids, I can tell you that I already have plenty of stress in my life, thank you very much. If de-cluttering will reduce it, I say let's give it a try.

So here's what I recommend: corral the kids into one area of the house, say the family room, their bedroom, or the basement. Make all toys stay there. Then, get rid of all the toys they don't play with. I tried to do this recently. I decided that the kids had too many stuffed animals. This realization came about when noticing that our older daughter spends all night sniffing because she's allergic to dust, while the younger stuffs these animals behind furniture when I tell her to clean up because their stuffed-animal hammock is overflowing.

So I surveyed their homely lot and chose twelve that the girls had not looked at since they were in diapers. I gathered them into several bags, hid the bags behind my back, and retreated quickly out the door. I threw them in the back of the van, where they would probably go unnoticed because of all the clutter. All was going fine until we headed out to the Salvation Army. It was then that I made my fatal mistake. I stopped at Dewe's first, where it was necessary to open the back of the van to retrieve the green boxes. Who should fall out but dear "Ellie" the Elephant and "Kitty," who jingles mercilessly when you shake her.

Katie promptly burst into tears, declaring Ellie and Kitty her most favoured possessions. I made her agree to get rid of the others, but Ellie and Kitty sat in prominence on her bed for three days. They have now fallen behind the bed (Katie has not noticed), and tonight, when they are asleep, I may try my kidnapping escapade again. But this time, I will not stop at Dewe's first.

## What Your Sock Drawer Says About You
*This column was first published November 3, 2003*

When walking through the mall last week I saw something inspiring. A man was pushing a baby carriage, inside of which was a baby wearing two different socks! One was pink, one was yellow, and they obviously did not come from the same pair.

Now perhaps this man is just clothing challenged when it comes to little girls. My husband, for instance, lives by the credo "girls' buttons always go at the back," which led to some very odd placement of bows and front collars on the rare occasions I actually allowed him to dress our daughters. He now lets them dress themselves, which is a whole other horror story.

I prefer to think that this stranger was not creating an inadvertent fashion faux pas but was instead being deliberate. I think he was trying to liberate himself from the stupidity of some of the customs we cling to. I currently have (I just checked) 4 pairs of socks in my drawer, 3 in each of the girls' drawers, 8 in my husband's, and 62 single socks in my stray sock drawer. If we were to mix and match, think of the money and frustration we could save!

That's not the only silly thing we do in our homes, though. Ironing has to rate high on that list, too. I stopped ironing a few years ago, as anyone who has ever seen my husband in dress shirts knows (he occasionally irons if we have to go somewhere fancy). When Rebecca was four, we were visiting the aunt who received the only neatness genes in my family. She was compulsively ironing a skirt. Rebecca stared, wide-eyed, and finally asked, "What are you doing?" She had never seen an iron before, though I would have preferred that she had kept that information to herself. Nevertheless, I now only buy knits and, in the process, save plenty of aggravation.

Then there's dusting. Dusting does not actually take very much time if you have little to dust. Wiping a cloth over a clear surface is a breeze. Dusting around thirty trophies that you won in grade four for some softball championship when you spent seven innings on the bench takes much more effort. So does dusting all those knick-knacks your in-laws bought you, the ones that cause you to wonder whether you have truly been accepted in the family yet or they're still trying to test you. I, of course, don't have any such knick-knacks, or at least I wouldn't admit to it after the fallout from that column last year about the annoying toys my mother-in-law buys for my girls. Suffice it to say that knick-knacks make dusting hard.

In fact, we could apply this principle to almost everything in our homes: stuff is your enemy. The more stuff you have, the less room you have for all the new stuff you're bringing into the house. Stuff soon piles up on your kitchen counter, your dining-room table, your front stairs, and soon you have stuff everywhere and you don't even know where to start cleaning. Throw stuff out, and you have room for the important things in your life.

Much of the problem with wasted effort around our homes, though, stems from the fact that we're aiming for the wrong thing. We want to have a perfect house to prove something to people. In the process, we end up compulsively dusting a living room no one ever sits in, to save it for company who, when they arrive, hang out in the kitchen anyway. Let's reclaim that space and aim for a comfortable home instead. Don't feel guilty if it's not perfect. Your house, after all, is meant to be lived in. And besides, there's no point getting stressed over housework that will never truly be finished anyway. I keep telling my kids that they can turn those matchless socks into sock puppets as soon as I've done all the laundry and I'm sure there's no stray ones there. But we all know the laundry is never finished. At the rate I'm going, those sock puppets will never see the light of day. Maybe it's time for some more liberation.

*The day after this column appeared, Keith was walking through the hospital when somebody looked at him, smirked, and said, "Nice shirt." Keith smiled as if to say "maybe you should go back on that medication" and tried to keep his distance. But the same thing happened in the elevator. And a nurse made a similar comment on the maternity floor. By this time, he knew something was up. He found the recycling bin, pulled out the previous day's paper, and found out I had told everyone his shirts weren't ironed. I still think that's pretty funny, but he may have other words for it.*

# Resolutions You Can Keep

*This column was first published December 30, 2003*

My husband is in the middle of changing his medical practice as of January 1, and I have a second book due in at the publisher the same day. So right now our lives are out of control, but next week everything will be different. Our time will once again be our own. This has caused us to do what everybody does this time of year: make New Year's resolutions about how much more disciplined we'll be as soon as the clock strikes midnight.

As parents, our resolutions usually concern our children. This year, I will not yell at my children (probable time until breakage: 2.3 days). I will not get behind on the laundry (4.2 days). I will exercise (1 day). I will organize creative crafts for my children every day (2 days). I will not eat my children's candy (1.5 days if said candy is chocolate, 17.8 days if not).

It's a losing proposition. We're trying to become someone we're never going to be. I recently got a new haircut that requires a little more blow-drying than usual. My 6-year-old sat me down this week and said, "Mommy, I think you should get your hair short again. You just can't handle this." And she's right. I'm chronically pressed for time, and if I try to do something too ambitious, I just feel guilty when I fail. Better to set the bar lower and be realistic.

This is not, however, how society works. I was asked to write an article for a large parenting magazine on indoor activities to do with your kids while it's raining. I came up with several suggestions, including, drink hot chocolate, bundle in some quilts, and play Monopoly, or pull out that video camera you always forget about and have the kids sing a song. Then the editor called. It seems I was horrendously mistaken. I was interpreting the assignment as follows: you're stuck in the house with really cranky kids who are fighting. You're desperate to find something to distract them before they drive you nuts, but you can't send them outside. So let's take this opportunity to have some fun doing things we keep putting off, and build our relationships in the process.

But modern parents aren't supposed to have these problems. We're all supposed to be super-creative, energetic cheerleaders. They changed my suggestions so they went something like this: Instead of playing Monopoly, let's get out the cardboard, paints, glue gun, papier mâché, plaster of Paris moulds, Mactac, heat-shrinkable wrap, decorative scissors, antique buttons, pop-can tabs, margarine lids, and MAKE YOUR OWN BOARD GAME! The kids come up with the theme, the rules, and the playing pieces, and then you all create it together.

And videotaping them singing, apparently, is also too tame. Instead, let's sew them some costumes as they practice a play with all the neighbourhood children, based on a classic novel you have recently read them. Once you have organized them into Chorus, Lead Roles, and Supporting Cast, they can create dialogue and choose props, such as everything you have in your garage, to create the play, which you will then videotape and give to all the neighbours.

I found myself wondering whose kids, exactly, they were talking about. Whenever you try to get any child I know to do a craft for more than five minutes, they lose interest, and you spend the next two hours grumpily putting it together yourself so you can display it and say, "Look what Johnny made!" And getting kids to agree who will be "Chorus" and who will be "Lead Role" is hardly a recipe for a stress-free afternoon. I decided this magazine wasn't in the business of helping parents; it was in the business of making parents feel inadequate.

Don't be a parent like that. Kids don't need props; they just need you to hug them and laugh with them. I do want to spend more time with my girls this year, but you won't catch me with any plaster of Paris. I'll be too busy drinking hot chocolate and playing Monopoly.

## The Family that Cleans Together
*This column was first published June 23, 2003*

When the bell rings at 3:15 this Wednesday, thousands of children will cheer lustily as they are released from their torment, though many parents may feel their torment is only beginning. Summer vacation is upon us. And why do we have summer vacation? It's not to give teachers a break; it's not because running in sprinklers is good for one's development; and it's not because the government doesn't want to pay to air condition the schools. No, it's because when public schooling started, children—yes, children—were needed to work on the farm.

The idea of kids working has fallen into disrepute, largely because for so long children, the most vulnerable in our society, were horrendously exploited. Whether sent into mines seven days a week in the last century or sold into indentured servitude in Asia today, children bear the brunt of economic misfortune. Yet being free from labour is not exactly the natural state of childhood, either. The idea that children should be completely free of responsibility until adulthood is new and, I think, potentially harmful.

I love knitting. And not just regular sweaters, but the kind that requires tiny needles, 35 colours, and four years to finish. When I do finally finish, I feel such a profound sense of accomplishment.

That feeling is something that is unique to being productive. We can feel something similar, though not nearly so thrilling, when we finally clean out the garage, or weed a large vegetable bed, or fix a leaky toilet (as long as it's not my husband doing it). Being productive gives you a sense that your labour matters and that you can spend it to help make life more livable, not just for you but also for your family.

> **The idea that children should be completely free of responsibility until adulthood is new and potentially harmful.**

To a large extent we have deprived our children of these experiences. Our fridge doors may be plastered with art "creations," but often this is as far as their productivity goes. The idea of actually helping with the dishes, for instance, is laughed off as the Nintendo is turned on.

Few children perform chores any more. In our parents' generation, kids would have had to help with the chores. It was expected, but it was also necessary. Now, most households can survive without the children's contribution, as long as the parents are willing to burn themselves out doing all the work.

But we're not only excusing them from chores; we're also turning our lives upside down to make theirs as easy and pleasant as possible. We rearrange our schedules to take kids to soccer, baseball, or the beach. We chauffeur them, clean them, feed them, and show them they are the centre of our universe. During the school year, in return, we may expect them to do homework. But summer is like two months of get-out-of-jail-free cards.

In the process, we're inadvertently contributing to children's propensity to being self-absorbed. The only thing they have to worry about is being a kid. And if we give them a chance to think their whole world revolves around their own cares and concerns, rather than the family's as a whole, things that really don't matter in the long run take on an ominous level of importance. Issues like who is your best friend, who has a crush on whom, or whom you get to sit beside at lunch can easily become way overblown. Chores aren't going to cure kids from worrying about these issues of preteen etiquette, but being responsible for things to benefit the whole family teaches kids that they are not prima donnas whom everyone else will serve.

Many of us are about to be blessed with our kids for two full months. Unless you want to spend all summer picking up popsicle wrappers and putting away beach toys, maybe it's time to introduce your kids to a toilet brush. They may not like it, but you'll be doing them a favour. They'll gain confidence and competence as they realize that this universe actually revolves around more people than just them. And then you may actually get a chance to put your own feet up and enjoy a popsicle yourself this summer.

*I try to write a column to launch each book that I write, and this was the one to launch* To Love, Honor and Vacuum. *I do make my kids do chores, though ironically we're much more organized during the school year than during the summer. We're just on the road too much in the summer for the girls to get all their chores done in one week. But then, I don't always get mine done, either, so I guess we all deserve a break. Now, if only I could get my garden to take care of itself, too...*

## The Perfect Trap
*This column was first published March 31, 2004*

f you turned on your television earlier this month, you could not escape the sight of Martha Stewart being found guilty of something (most of us aren't really sure of what). When listening to a juror discuss the case, though, what was clear is that Martha's biggest fault was that she just wasn't likeable.

Martha made us feel like inconsequential slugs because she could pull off perfect without breaking a sweat. This woman would go for a walk in the woods and find inspiration in pine cones. She would collect them, spray-paint them, stick white parchment with guests' names in golden calligraphy on them, and bravo, have brand new place settings. Had you or I been in the woods, we would have been too busy listening to the birds to notice the hidden potential in pines. That's our problem, you see. We're too busy living to be good housekeepers.

But that doesn't stop us from feeling guilty that our homes are chaotic. We huddle indoors, afraid to let anybody in for fear they may notice how we actually live. We may meet a neighbour and want to invite her in for coffee, only to realize to our horror that our breakfast dishes are still in the sink. Instead, we wave and retreat inside again where we can turn on the gardening channel and find out how awful our front yards look.

Don't get me wrong. I love gardening. I even like some of Martha's crafts. But we can go way overboard on this need to have perfect homes. We forget what homes are really about.

In the end, relationships matter. Dust bunnies don't. That doesn't mean we shouldn't clean, simply that when we do our aim is to create a comfortable home where everybody will want to be, not a perfect home where we get nervous if the kids play. My grandmother used to lament the fact that she couldn't keep her home perfect like some of her neighbours could. But one day she woke up to the reason. She always had children over. She had toys. She had books. She had magazines. Her friends had collections of floor polish.

Yet which was more of a home? The one where you could see your reflection on the floor or the one where you could see your child's latest Lego creation? A home will contain toys, books, crafts, and hobbies, all of which are evidence of the personalities who live there. There's nothing wrong with that. After all, we invite people over to get to know us anyway. If you get to know me, you also get to know my knitting. And the books I'm reading. And my daughters' attempts to make little cats out of cotton balls. Everybody's more comfortable in a house that reflects you than in an antiseptically clean house straight out of *Better Homes and Gardens.*

Sometimes we forget this lesson. Think about what your children heard you say today. Many days at my house, it's things like "What are your toys doing on the stairs?" "Get your stuff out of the living room! Do you expect me to always clean it up?" "Why can't you ever pick anything up?" Add all this up, and the message is clear: "You kids are a hassle. Shape up!"

I want our house to be comfortable. That means my kids must be allowed to play. It also needs to be comfortable for me, though, so they can't play where I want to knit. And they do have to keep their piles to a minimum so we can all walk without breaking our necks. A comfortable home also means being able to shower without fear of contracting some disease. Cleanliness and basic clutter control are both certainly necessary. Perfection, though, is not.

Sometimes I forget these lessons, and the yelling begins again. But housework does not make a home. People do. My house will never be perfect, but I hope it's one that my children will one day look back on fondly. I think it's time to get out the cotton balls and try for some bunnies, just in time for Easter.


## Food Fights

*This column was first published April 21, 2003*

*A*fter a recent column imploring stay-at-home moms to give themselves a break, a reader e-mailed me to thank me. She had been exhausting herself trying to create the perfect home, complete with "irresistible" dinners for the family, and she was running out of steam.

Preparing "irresistible" dinners, though, is not really our problem. We all know how to do that: ketchup with hotdogs on the side, followed by ice cream, ice cream, and more ice cream. For kids (especially mine), ketchup is its own food group. When my oldest daughter Rebecca was little, she would dip her french fries in it and lick it off, never actually consuming said fry until it was a slobbery mess, at which point she would graciously offer it to me.

Irresistible, then, isn't hard. But preparing healthy food that kids actually want to eat is. The simple fact is that healthy isn't fun, and there are so much more appealing foods readily available. When our first was born, we read all the baby books that told us there was no need to introduce sugar until they were two. But the book forgot to warn us about grandparents, and sure enough, our child had ice cream and chocolate galore long before her second birthday. Part of the joy of being a grandparent, after all, is making kids happy without having to be the responsible ones. I can hardly wait to have grandchildren myself, but in the meantime I'm stuck trying to convince my kids that broccoli can be just as appealing as ice cream.

Kids see right through this. One reader wrote me about a time she was trying to convince her son that this particular green vegetable would indeed tantalize the tastebuds. "Look, honey, Mommy and Daddy like our broccoli," she said, as they both dutifully lifted their forks to their mouths. Their son peered at them suspiciously.

"Yeah, but which of you wants seconds?" Kids get smart way too early.

It's not only that kids reject the healthy stuff. They turn their noses up at the way it's served, too. My children, for instance, cannot eat anything if it is actually touching anything else. So if we have stew, and I want them to actually eat it, I have to separate out the meat and the carrots and the potatoes, so they don't contaminate one another.

But even if you do everything right, kids still eye the food suspiciously. Very early in life they develop strategies for how to consume the least amount of "gross" food as possible. Rebecca refuses to eat anything that looks like it has a spice or an herb in it. So she'll painstakingly remove all the green flecks of parsley off something and eat the rest, consuming approximately 8.5% of any given item and leaving the remainder in minuscule pieces all over her plate.

With all these strategies, how do we get kids to actually eat? Don't give them a choice. I don't make them actually eat (I remember too well eating stuff that I honestly thought was going to make me vomit), but I don't give them anything else, either. They just go hungry if they don't eat their dinner. This means, of course, that snacks in the house must be kept to a minimum. If kids know that if they don't eat their dinner, two hours later they can demolish a bag of chips in front of the TV, dinner will seem even less attractive. But if snacks consist of only fruit or vegetables, dinner suddenly may not seem so bad.

If that's too drastic, you can try what some of my friends do: offer them a once-weekly "out." Let them know they can choose a hot dog and an apple for one meal—but only one—each week. If they hate Monday's dinner, they have to figure out if there's a possibility Thursday's might be even worse.

Struggles over food are almost universal, yet miraculously most kids grow out of this picky stage. While they're in it, just stick to your guns. The more you do, the more you'll be able to drown out all the *EWWWW*s and sit back and enjoy your meal. Even the broccoli.


## A Growing Concern
*This column was first published October 27, 2003*

How does one start a column about childhood obesity? That it's a huge problem? That it's a growing concern? You can hardly mention it without causing snickers. Recent studies, though, show that this problem will not go away unless we start taking it seriously. Over one in five children is now obese, let alone all the kids who qualify as overweight.

You may argue that the health risks of obesity are overrated. After all, my father-in-law's family for generations practised lives that would make Health Canada bureaucrats have apoplexy, but they all lived to a ripe old age. He would say this had something to do with their minds not being poisoned by rooting for the Maple Leafs, though I think the answer is that some people just have incredibly lucky genes. Most of us, though, do not.

If we're overweight, we're far more likely to die early. Even if we don't, our lives will be more difficult. We'll have less energy. We'll get sick more often. We're more likely to be depressed.

For children, the effects are perhaps even worse, because of the social cost. I will never forget Edmund, a boy from my fourth-grade class. None of the other boys wanted to be his friend. Edmund, you see, was the only one in our class who was overweight. If you were to look into a grade-four classroom today, though, there would probably be at least three or four kids larger than Edmund was.

What is going to happen to these kids? Like Edmund, they're likely to be ostracized. But that's not all. Those who suffer shame like this are less likely to go on to higher education, more likely to get involved in destructive behaviour, and more likely, if female, to become single mothers.

Schools can lecture kids on proper nutrition all they want, but this will only go so far, because schools do not do your grocery shopping. Ultimately, the answer lies with parents. Many parents complain that it's hard to get kids to lose weight, and they're right. But children have one thing going for them that we adults do not: they grow. It's much easier to knock off those harmful pounds now than it will be in twenty years, and make no mistake about it—they will have to do it sooner or later.

The reason losing weight is hard is not because it's rocket science. We gain weight because we eat too much and we don't move enough. To lose weight, reverse the equation. What's hard about it is that children, who like their cakes and cookies and TV, will resist. This does not mean, though, that you should wave the white flag in defeat. Instead, recite to yourself, several times a day, "I am the parent." After all, do you want your kids to love you, or do you want to love them? If you let them do what they want, they will love you (though this love may not last). But this is not acting lovingly. To act lovingly is to take care of your kids, even if it means stopping them from doing something harmful that they enjoy.

So unplug the television set. Sitting on the couch watching TV burns fewer calories than sitting on the couch staring at a blank TV screen. And when kids are watching TV, they like to eat. Unplug the TV, and they'll do something else, even if they complain for a while.

Then, empty out your cupboards. There is absolutely no reason why chips, pop, sugary cereals, candy bars, or Twinkies need to be in your house. Certainly they can be treats every now and then, but no child needs more than one or two small treats a day.

It's easy to make excuses when our kids are big, but this is becoming a national health crisis that, for our kids' sakes, we can't afford to ignore. Instead of letting kids collapse in front of the TV and demolish a bag of chips, let's start taking walks after dinner. You'll get some exercise, and you'll grow your relationship at the same time. Besides, as my father-in-law would attest, it's infinitely better than sitting at home and rooting for the Leafs.

*My father-in-law loves it when I can get any Leaf bashing into columns. Since I really don't care either way, I'm happy to oblige.*

## Saving Dinner
*This column was first published November 24, 2003*

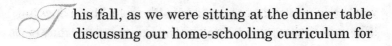his fall, as we were sitting at the dinner table discussing our home-schooling curriculum for

the upcoming year, I had an all-too-vivid reminder that we had neglected a vital part of our daughters' education. My children eat like neanderthals. They can't sit still, they slurp, they use their fingers, they interrupt, they reach, and yes, as you learned last week, they fart. How could this happen? Where did we go wrong? When I was little, I remember my mother saying things like "Sheila, sit up straight" or "Remember to use your knife." Today, I find myself saying "Rebecca, stay in your chair" and "Remember to use your fork."

Somewhere along the line we forgot to teach our kids the polite way to eat. Once they had mastered picking up the food themselves and getting most of it in their mouths rather than in their hair, we figured our job had ended. It's not that I don't think manners are important, though; I think perhaps it's because as a culture, we've made dinner a far more casual affair than it once was.

Families used to eat dinner together, and not just once or twice a week but all the time. Today we eat McDonald's drive-through on our way to errands, if we're lucky. One recent study from the University of Minnesota found that most families eat together only three times a week, and those meals take far less time than they did even twenty years ago. We sit down, we inhale, we get up.

> Somewhere along the line we forgot to teach our kids the polite way to eat.

That's too bad, because studies also show that eating together has incredible benefits. Teens who eat dinner with their families at least five times a week are less likely to do drugs or be depressed and are more likely to do well in school. And kids who never eat with their parents are 60% more likely to smoke or drink. It only makes sense; dinner is one of those few opportunities to all be together and actually talk. At other times, we're running in different directions. Dinner is a time to catch up, to talk about what we're worried about and what we're happy about, and just to connect. And the more we connect, the more likely we are to have good relationships with our kids. Besides that, if we have dinner together, we're more likely to spend time together after dinner. We may pull out the Monopoly game, do a puzzle, or read a book.

Unfortunately, with shift work becoming more and more common, making time to eat together is difficult. On the nights when my husband is working, I find it hard to get excited about cooking a meal. After all, chances are my kids won't like it anyway, and why cook just for me? Dinner, instead of becoming a family tradition where we all meet at the table, becomes haphazard, depending on who is where on any given night.

Traditions seem old-fashioned, but this is one we should fight to preserve. We need that time all together. If your spouse isn't there, you can still try to make the effort to sit down with your kids, even if it's just around a bowl of Corn Flakes and some scrambled eggs. One of my New Year's resolutions is to make dinners more important family occasions (more about that in January). We've now started to bring out the good dishes, even for regular meals. My kids love drinking their orange juice out of wine glasses, and it seems to inspire them to concentrate more on manners. We've even begun to light candles, which aside from delighting my children has the fortunate side effect of rendering the "yucky green stuff" Mommy puts on food—in other words, the parsley—a little less visible. It also creates an ambience where farting is not as natural an occurrence.

We're still left with that pesky problem, though, that when it comes to utensils my kids do eat like pigs, except that pigs will eat anything and my kids will not. So between now and January, I am going to teach my girls to eat like little ladies. Wish me luck.

*Our kids are slowly getting better, though it's still a struggle. But then, my mother is still trying to get me to sit up straight, and I'm 34. By the way, you can find the farting column on page 45.*

## Preventing the 5:30 Panic
*This column was first published January 19, 2004*

Without a doubt, the worst place to be at 5:30 p.m. on a weeknight is standing in line at the grocery store with kids. They're cranky; you're cranky; everybody's hungry; and all around you are people in the same position.

This 5:30 ritual naturally follows from the 5:00 one, whereby you stand in the middle of your kitchen hoping for some inspiration. You open your freezer and are greeted by packages of fish sticks and pizza, each containing only one, covering up the liver you bought in a health frenzy 27 months ago. You decide it's easier to start fresh.

When we think about parenting, we often focus on improving communication, effective discipline, or even instilling values. Yet just as important—if not more so—are the relationship dividends that come from leisurely eating and talking together regularly. In a column a few weeks ago, I talked about how family dinners are one of the few times that this communication can naturally occur. Eating dinner is central to keeping up with your kids, helping them academically, and even teaching the art of silent flatulence. But these precious moments will be lost if dinner is harried and chaotic.

A few months ago I took my own advice and started planning my meals (I had to; I told people in my book they were supposed to, so I figured I'd better, too). And you know what? I was right! Planning meals does make a big difference. Know what you're going to make and who's going to cook it, and you eliminate the last-minute guessing games. I was even given a book called *Saving Dinner* by Leanne Ely, which gives 32 weeks of meal plans, recipes, and grocery lists so you don't even have to think (a big plus). Armed with that book, my husband and I went to the grocery store and bought a week's worth of groceries to follow her plan.

There was only one problem. We came home and had nowhere to put all this food. Our cupboards were too full, and our kitchen is rather small. As we were discussing this conundrum while washing the pots after dinner, Keith had what was, to him, a flash of brilliance.

"Doing dishes together is so relaxing," he said. "Why don't we take out the dishwasher altogether and then put in more cupboards? We'd have more room."

Ten minutes later, after I had stopped spluttering

and was able to climb up off of the floor, I replied, "You know, honey, we could connect just as well by snuggling while *listening* to the dishwasher. Besides, we don't need more cupboards. We just need to eat more!"

Not all at once, mind you. But think of the money you have invested in your cupboards and freezer. Five-year-old Jell-O mixes? Cranberry sauce? Soups? I even have three different kinds of lentils. We buy these things on impulse with no clear plan about what we're going to do with them, and they just end up sitting there. What we do with produce is even worse. Most of it can better be called a science experiment. We fill up our carts with all these lovely green things, only to have them turn into runny brown things. One could argue that this can be used for family togetherness—"Let's play 'What Was It?'"—but it's probably better not to waste money like this in the first place.

So for the next few weeks, our family is going to eat through our house. It may make for some interesting meals (cranberry sauce, fish, and Jell-O), but we probably won't have to spend much on groceries for at least two months, enough time to pay off all those Christmas bills. Then we can start this meal planning in earnest. We'll buy only what we need for this week, and what we will buy, we will actually eat. Of course, we'll still have to keep on hand extra for "company" meals and snacks. We'll keep our basic supply of baking goods, cereals, and any necessary chocolate, too, but that's it. I can keep my dishwasher; I won't stand in line at the last minute; and we can relax over dinner like we're supposed to. But I think I'll toss that liver.

# My Summer Grocery Cart

*This column was first published August 9, 2004*

*I* hate grocery shopping in the summer. The shopping itself is not the problem. It's the possibility of meeting somebody I know in the checkout line. You know that little routine; you probably do it yourself. There you stand, with your cart filled with chips, hot dogs, ice cream, popsicles, and pop galore, and you try to arrange the one bag of romaine lettuce so it hides the Twinkies. "It's for the kids, you know," you say, knowing full well you'll consume more than half of the stuff yourself.

I eat horribly in the summer. So does my family. It's not intentional, exactly; it's just that when you're at the beach, or out camping, or going on a picnic, it's so much easier to grab a bag of chips than it is to make a fruit salad. My kids absolutely adore summer, and it's not just because of the swimming. For once they don't have to beg for the Fruit Roll Ups or the ice cream sandwiches to no avail, because I actually say yes. I know you can pack healthy foods for a picnic, and two or three times in the summer I actually try. When we go camping, we do start out with a lot of fruit and vegetables, but by about the third or fourth day these are all gone and the chips are popping out again.

During the school year I am preoccupied with those 5-10 servings of vegetables and fruits a day we all are supposed to eat. I count fibre grams on the cereal boxes. But I love summer and cracking open bags of granola bars with marshmallows and chocolate chips in them, which the kids usually only get from their grandma.

Naturally, I feel a tad guilty about this, but I figure the kids are running around so much they're at least burning off a lot of calories. What really amazes me, however, is how expensive my summer grocery bill is. It's not just the chips and pretzels, either; cooking with Hamburger Helper or store-bought marinade packets, our camping staples that I never buy normally, sure makes that bill add up.

> What really amazes me, however, is how expensive my summer grocery bill is.

I simply do not know how people afford groceries if they buy prepared foods all the time. I once heard that, for a healthy diet, you should spend 90% of your money on the outer aisles of the grocery store: the breads, the dairy, the fruits and vegetables, and the meats. Normally I never venture into those inner aisles, except for flour or to feed my Diet Pepsi craving. And that's probably why we usually only spend about $90 a week on groceries for the four of us. It's not expensive if you're making food from scratch.

Increasingly, though, people don't do this. First, many of us were never taught how to cook from scratch. We simply don't know how. Yet even if we do know, it can be hard to find the time or the energy. The other seems so much easier. And it is. But it's not healthy, and it's sure hard on your wallet.

This year I'm starting to teach my 9-year-old how to make some simple suppers, including spaghetti and chicken pie. Neither is difficult, and she's feeling very grown-up knowing that she can actually cook. The next step is to make twice as much and freeze half, so that when we are pressed for time, we're not tempted towards those other aisles.

My husband, when he had his office practice, often had parents complain that a healthy diet was just too expensive. That, however, is a common misperception. Certainly fruits and vegetables can seem expensive (although they're never cheaper than they will be right now during the summer), but think how much more two apples will fill you up than a whole bag of chips. You don't need to buy as much food if you're eating healthily as you do if you're depending on starches to fill your diet.

I'll try to remember this when I'm stocking up for my next camping trip. But I probably won't completely return to my winter ways just yet. So if you happen to see me in the grocery store, and I pretend not to notice you, just don't look in my shopping cart.

*My sister-in-law Tina first gave me the idea for this column when we were sitting at the beach with all the kids and laughing about all the junk we were letting them eat. There's no real excuse, we decided. But sometimes, junk is just fun.*

# Keeping Love Alive

When we think about parenting, we focus on "raising kids," but we really should change that perspective. We should be raising families. Children will always fare better when their parents have a great marriage. Besides that, one day the children will leave, and you two will be left behind. If you don't encourage that primary relationship now, even during the busy years, you could have awfully lonely retirement years ahead of you.

I do, however, find it difficult writing these columns knowing that so many single parents are struggling with the breakdown of their own relationships and the dearth of prospects for new ones. I certainly don't want anybody to feel guilty. I do want to challenge and encourage, not to hit someone on the head. My own mother was a single mother, and I know how difficult and lonely that can be. I hope I achieve the right balance with these columns on navigating romance when kids enter the picture.

## My Man of Steel
*This column was first published December 16, 2002*

This Saturday I'm supposed to give my husband something made of steel. We're celebrating our eleventh anniversary, and for this blessed occasion whoever is in charge of anniversary gift etiquette obviously ran out of ideas. "Paper? Taken. A nice wooden chest? Taken. What about diamonds? Better save that as an incentive to stick around." Growing increasingly desperate, she probably looked out the window, saw her husband's '57 Chevy up on blocks, and yelled, "Steel!" forever relegating us to eleventh anniversary hopelessness.

I figure I'm left with a new car (fat chance), the foundation for a new house, or power tools. But the only thing more ridiculous than me trying to choose a power tool would be my husband trying to use one. The one and only time he did any home improvements was his attempt, along with another doctor friend, to hang a pot rack. Instead of drilling into a stud, they drilled into my toilet drain, sending water—and I don't know what else—into our kitchen.

> Indeed, that idea—that love keeps us together—can actually harm a relationship.

Whatever I choose, though, it occurs to me that Ye Olde Marriage Etiquette Lady may have had a point.

Steel is an appropriate metaphor for marriage. Steel holds houses together, keeps bridges from buckling, and forms the foundations of our cities. Steel doesn't bend.

Over the years of our marriage we've had some tough times. Keith's residency at the Hospital for Sick Children was horrendous. He always came home exhausted. Two babies demanded our attention, leaving us with no energy for anything else. In the middle of this, we had a beautiful baby boy, who lived only 29 days. Though I will treasure those precious four weeks forever, his death left a hole that can never be filled on this side of heaven.

When I walked down the aisle eleven years ago, I knew I loved Keith and that he loved me. I figured that love would be enough for forever. I was wrong. Love alone would not have seen us through these eleven years, through miscarriages and sleepless nights, through baby stresses and our son's death. As much as I adore my husband, I don't think it's love that has made our marriage strong. Indeed, that idea—that love keeps us together—can actually harm a relationship.

If love is what keeps us together, then when we stop feeling all gushy towards each other we wonder if the relationship is viable. Commitment is just as important as love, and perhaps even more so. If you're not truly committed to each other, you can't really discuss problems. Whenever you do, the whole relationship may be at stake. But when you are committed to each other, you can hash something out until you get it right, because you know that person isn't going anywhere.

During our first year of marriage, I was ready to kill my husband many times over, or at least bean him on the head with a frying pan. He understood nothing about my feelings, while I, of course, understood everything about his. What allowed us to get through that time was not that we loved each other—there were times we both doubted it—but that we knew we were in this for the long haul. And if you're in it for the long haul, then you may as well work it out, because the longer you wait, the more miserable you're going to be.

In every relationship there are times when splitting up seems like the only option. Certainly in situations of abuse or chronic infidelity this may be the case. But overall, I believe that most people will be happier if they choose to stay and work it out. And then your kids will feel free to explore and to grow, because they know their anchor to the world, their family, is secure.

My husband is the most romantic guy in the world. He's easy to love. And as we've chosen to commit to each other, the steel holding up our house has grown stronger. My kids can tear all over it and it won't collapse. They can jump and tug and pull, and we'll stand firm. I cherish every day we have together, and I look forward to many more.

*After this column appeared, my husband was attending a Caesarean section. All was quiet in the room when suddenly the obstetrician said, "Isn't he just so sweet?" and all the nurses laughed. He still says it's the column that embarrassed him the most. But he really doesn't mind.*

## Are We Having Fun Yet?
*This column was first published February 17, 2003*

ast Friday night, Chapters was probably bustling. It was Valentine's Day, so it would have been filled with couples determined to have some fun because they had babysitters at home, and gosh darnit, they were going to have a night out if it killed them.

Last year, my husband and I dutifully hired a sitter, left the house at 6:00, and went to a lovely restaurant, where we proceeded to have a lovely dinner and a lovely conversation. But we were finished by 7:30, even with the dessert and the coffee. So then what should we do? It was way too early to go home, so we headed, like many other desperate couples, to Chapters. There we sipped another coffee and leafed through magazines, trying to pretend we were having a romantic time while surreptitiously checking our watches to see when it would be okay to go home.

The alternative to Chapters is a movie. That's a little more likely this year, because there are a few half-decent ones out, but last year was disastrous. The only truly great movie of 2002 was, in my opinion, *My Big Fat Greek Wedding*. It was marriage affirming, family affirming, and side-splittingly funny. We saw it eight months after it had first been released, and the movie theatre was still so packed we had to sit in the second row, giving our necks a major kink. It put that line in the movie "the husband is the head of the house, and the wife is the neck that turns him" in an entirely different perspective.

For whatever reason, Hollywood insists on making movies as if every moviegoer is a hormonally charged 17-year-old who thinks that flatulence is an art form and that no movie is complete without car chases. I find this curious, since the most profitable movies tend to be ones that deal with relationships. *My Big Fat Greek Wedding*, for instance, cost only $5 million to make and has already grossed over $200 million at the theatres, before it's even out on video. Most movies put out by the regular studios, though, actually *lose* money, because real people don't want to watch them. (Hollywood, it seems, has a shortage of real people, or they would have figured this out before sinking $175 million into *Waterworld*.)

Hollywood's steady stream of drivel, though, is not the only reason many of us avoid movies. We arrive at the theatres, and what is the first thing we parents look at? It isn't the *titles* of the movies; it's the *time* they start. We know that if we're up too late we'll pay for it tomorrow, because our little ones will have no sympathy for us and will still insist on crying periodically throughout the night or jumping on us at one in the morning. We're so chronically tired that everything revolves around the clock.

So last year, Keith and I didn't go to a movie, and Chapters eventually closed. We decided to drive down to Zwick's and just talk before setting the sitter free. Unfortunately, other people in that vicinity had other plans for the night. Soon after arriving in the parking lot, another car joined us, and a portly man, about 60, stared into our van. At first we were wondering if it was some sort of drug deal, but he looked a little old. Then he climbed out of his car and walked around to ours, staring at Keith a little funny. Keith roared off in reverse, and, defeated, we went home. A while later the police department announced that they had arrested several men for soliciting (and performing) sex acts in that particular park.

Yes, the state of romance for married couples with small children is indeed very bleak. This year, we didn't do anything for Valentine's Day, because we were away. But next year, I know what I'll do. I'll organize with some friends to hire a babysitter who can watch all our kids at her house. Then each of us couples will go out individually for a nice dinner, rent a movie that we choose ourselves, go home, cuddle on the couch to watch it, and still be asleep by 10:30. Now that's romance, and it sounds pretty good to me.

## Who Do You Love?

*(I know that grammatically the title should be "Whom Do You Love?" Whom, though, sounds pretentious, so the editors and I changed it. Sorry.)*

*This column was first published February 10, 2003*

Yesterday a mouse died on my kitchen floor. I'm not sure exactly how. When I went to prepare breakfast for my kids, it wasn't there. But when my kids went to toss what remained of their breakfast into the garbage (probably enough to feed a small country), great screams erupted, creating a racket I soon added to when I caught a glimpse of the lifeless rodent myself. My only explanation is that when I was opening and closing the cupboards, it must have stuck its head out, at which point I slammed the door and broke its neck.

It reminds me of an incident last summer when the girls and I were emptying out of one of our compost bins. After I had thrust the shovel into the compost, what should fall down but six writhing, pink, hairless baby mice. They tumbled out of the bin, and once again screaming started, much to the delight of our neighbours, who were retiling their roof and watching from above as the three of us jumped up and down like we were being attacked by yellow jackets.

The mother mouse, however, did not share their enjoyment. She screamed, and I mean *screamed* (I didn't know mice could). Then she darted between our feet, looking petrified up at us as she carried off each of her offspring in turn.

That mouse risked her life to save her babies. She needn't have bothered; I was far too squeamish to finish them off (though I may inadvertently do so in my kitchen). But what she did was perfectly natural. Almost every animal mother in the world will risk life and limb to save her babies. The only animal mothers who will allow their offspring to be hurt are humans.

I am reminded of this at Valentine's Day by the story of a mother who, in 2000, won the kissing contest at the Quinte Mall. The object of her affections was her fiancé, the father of her unborn child, who had, the previous summer, shaken her older son Tyler to death (the fiancé eventually served time for this). Killing her son, it seems, was not enough to render him ineligible as husband material. To be fair, she didn't believe he had done the deed, and she did eventually leave him. But her denial of the truth is, sadly, all too common.

Too many of us women are so desperate for affection that we would choose a man over our own children. Susan Smith did that in the United States a few years ago when she drove her boys into a lake, still strapped in their car seats, because her new boyfriend didn't want kids.

Choosing a partner is a difficult task. Many of us feel incomplete without a man, and we're so desperate for companionship we'll take anyone who comes our way. We fret incessantly, "Does he like me? Does he really like me?" but we forget to ask, "Do I like him?" If women only chose men who treated us with respect, though, the incidence of woman abuse would go down the toilet.

Hard as it is to choose a man initially, it's even harder when you already have children. Yet this is when it's even more crucial to have our eyes wide open. Studies show that stepfathers, like little Tyler's "dad," are more than three times as likely to abuse their stepchildren than are natural fathers and more than five times as likely to sexually abuse stepdaughters.

Does that mean single mothers should give up hope? Not at all. Many stepfathers, including some in my own extended family, are as loving as any father could be. But our primary concern needs to be for our kids, future or otherwise. They aren't able to choose. We have to choose for them, so we had better do it right.

No guy is worth putting up with abuse for, of either you or your kids. And no guy is worth giving up your kids for. We don't have to explain that to mice. We do have to explain it to too many women. This Valentine's Day, let's concentrate not on making sure we're loved romantically but on making sure we love appropriately.

*Little Tyler's death had a big impact on my husband and me, coming at the beginning of his practice in Belleville. Tyler was almost exactly my daughter Katie's age, and I still think of him every now and then and mourn for his grandparents. Such things should never happen to a child. I hope that women everywhere will start making better choices so that such people will never be allowed anywhere near our children. And, if we ourselves are the problem, I hope we have enough love to get some help.*

# Who Is Marriage Really For?
*(Here's another of those grammatically incorrect titles. Again, "For Whom Is Marriage?" just sounds pretentious. Sorry.)*

*This column was first published August 11, 2003*

People have asked my opinion on gay marriage, so I've decided to wade into the debate, and I'll likely get caught way up to my neck with what I'm about to write. But first, I think "gay" marriage is the wrong starting point. We're debating homosexuality, which is unfortunate because it's caused hurt when it's really a side issue. The main issue is marriage.

The purpose of marriage is to keep the fragile bonds of the family from fraying. It's to build a link between people that is difficult to break, and thus insulate the children, and indeed the whole family, from disruption. And it's proven remarkably adept at doing that.

People who are married are happier, healthier, live longer, and earn more money. (They also have more satisfying sex lives!) They suffer less depression, less substance abuse, and fewer instances of suicide. Children whose parents divorce, on the other hand, are more depressed, do worse in school, and experience more poverty and abuse. Even among upper-class white families, children whose parents divorce have a 25% chance of experiencing serious social, emotional, or psychological problems twenty years down the road (double the risk of intact families) and are five times more likely, if girls, to become teenage mothers. The stress from divorce even seems to affect our bodies. Thirty-five percent of girls whose parents divorce start menstruating before age 12, compared with 18% in intact families. These kids are also twice as likely to drop out of school and to become chronic criminal offenders. Marriage matters.

This is not to suggest, however, that *all* kids whose parents are married will do better than *all* kids in single-parent homes. Many single parents do remarkable jobs with their kids, while many married parents are horrible. On an individual basis, we can defy statistics. But on a society-wide basis, marriage wins every time.

Society, then, has a vested interest in preserving marriage. Instead, we're eroding it. We loosened divorce laws because we believed that parents' happiness was of primary importance to children's happiness, though research has yet to bear this out.

But not only have we allowed commitments to be easily broken, we also have eliminated the requirement of commitment as we treat those who cohabit the same as those who marry. Naturally, some cohabiting couples will raise children together well. But statistically, cohabiting relationships are inherently more unstable than marriages, leaving children—and women—often worse off. Keeping sex and commitment linked provided protection for women. Women bear the costs of relationships gone sour, as they are the ones left pregnant or caring for kids. Now it's harder to obtain commitment, since all the "benefits" are available without it.

In the process, we're defining sexual relationships in terms of what *we* want rather than what is best for the kids. Proponents of gay marriage often argue that kids shouldn't be a factor, anyway; after all, not all hetero-sexual marriages have children. But this misses the point. Over thousands of years, society evolved hetero-sexual marriage to protect that type of relationship—the only one capable of creating children. Whether or not an individual couple did produce children was irrelevant. By keeping these relationships committed, we ensured that whenever there was the potential for children, these kids would be protected.

Marriage fundamentally was not about only two people. That's a modern construct. It was about creating a safe, secure environment for the family. Now we hear cries to open up marriage to a variety of different rela-tionships in the name of civil rights, as if it's an issue of discrimination. But marriage was never about rights; it was about responsibilities. Once we make it about rights, we change the definition of marriage entirely. Gay mar-riage is only the final straw signalling that marriage is now about adult wishes rather than children's needs.

Many of us are desperately trying to choose commit-ment for our kids as we keep our marriages together, search for a proper partner, or teach our kids to choose their own mates well. But if we further erode marriage, what are we choosing for our grandchildren? We are creating a society where kids are only a secondary con-sideration. I think it's time we figure out how to put their needs first once again.

*This was probably the hardest column I ever wrote.*
*I was trying to make a coherent argument without*
*being judgmental, and in retrospect I still like it.*
*It's been published a number of other times in the*

States, and I've received plenty of e-mail on it, both supportive and angry. This is a huge issue to me, though. The disintegration of marriage will hurt kids, and you don't have to be a genius to see that it already has. I don't want marriage to become just another lifestyle choice, because as soon as we make it into a choice, it becomes one that fewer and fewer people will make. I'm not sure how to stop the slide now, but I mourn the direction we are going in, and I pray that things will turn around again.

# The Custody Blues
*This column was first published July 21, 2003*

Summer vacation may bring to mind beaches, camping, and sun, but to me it often brings back memories of something far more horrible: child custody arrangements. As a kid, the only time I would see my father was for a few weeks every summer.

So I've been mulling over custody lately, and I've come to some conclusions. I think joint custody should be automatic in all divorce settlements, except where it can be shown that this is not in the best interests of the child. Children need both parents, and it's awfully hard to be a parent just on the weekends.

Can parenting really be condensed into only a few days every month? It needs to happen regularly, to build up trust so that kids can share, learn, and listen to your discipline and your advice. When kids are separated from a parent, they begin to lead completely different lives, so that when they join together, they often have little in common. In too many families, these visits have to become "events," because sitting around at home feels awkward. The child has essentially lost one parent, and in many cases of sole custody, the child loses out on grandparents, aunts and uncles and cousins, too.

That being said, I also don't think joint custody is easily workable. When people divorce, they obviously have problems with one another. To expect those to automatically disappear and to focus on the children may be ideal, but it isn't simple. "But Dad doesn't make me do chores!" "But Mom says I don't have to keep taking piano if I don't want to!" "Dad lets me stay up until 9:30." The struggles are endless.

In fact, I'm grateful my mother had sole custody. I wasn't confused by constantly shuffling back and forth. When I did have to see my dad, all the feelings of rejection came flooding back, but on a day-to-day basis I could ignore them.

The reason this was better for me, though, is not that joint custody itself is bad. It's because what kids need is not custody arrangements that work but parents who both want to parent. There is nothing worse for a child than to be stood up by a parent. It's Dad's weekend, but he can't come because he's too busy. Mom has me every Wednesday, but it's too much of a strain on her schedule to break up her week. Trying to explain why Daddy isn't coming again or why Mommy had to work again is heartbreaking for the parent left behind, too. In such cases, I think it's far better to give up the pretext of "joint custody" or even "frequent visitation." It's better to be like my father, seeing children only sporadically, so that the relationship doesn't hurt on such a regular basis.

Frankly, if you don't want to see your kids, then you don't deserve to parent. Your children should come first. If they don't, you've failed at the most important task in your life. You should either make the decision to change and to love your children or you should let them get on with their lives.

So to recap, sole custody is bad, and so, often, is joint custody. What's the solution? I really don't think there's an easy one. The only thing that will keep us from heartache is to be smart at the start: only marry someone you can picture staying with your whole life; don't have children with jerks; and, except in cases of abuse, addiction, or affairs, stay married.

If your marriage has already broken up and you're struggling with custody, I know it's hard, and please know I don't intend to lay a guilt trip. Many single parents out there do a wonderful job, and I applaud them! Just keep focusing on what your kids need, and don't get bogged down by all the "what ifs" of how your life could have turned out. But for everyone else, remember: splitting up will not necessarily make your life better, and it will often make your children's lives worse. It's easier to work your problems through. So please try. Kids would be a lot better off without the rejection that divorces often bring.

## Valentine's Day Prescription
*This column was first published February 9, 2004*

When you're married, Valentine's Day seems more like a duty than a holiday. You already have a Valentine, which is a great relief, but can also be a challenge. Can you keep love alive after you've already heard your beloved make every disgusting bodily noise there is?

For those who are single, I know Valentine's Day can be difficult. If you're raising kids alone and putting them first, you are one of the best models of love there is. Forgive me for concentrating on married couples here, but we do need some help. Marriages aren't doing very well, which is tragic because marriage is so beneficial. In *The Case for Marriage*, Maggie Gallagher and Linda Waite quote statistic after statistic that show that by virtue of being married, you're likely to live longer, make more money, be happier, be healthier, have better sex, and have better relationships in all areas of your life. And those are just the benefits for *us*. The benefits for our kids are just as dramatic.

> Let's remember that we're not just raising kids, we're raising families.

The best gift we can give our children, then, is to nurture our marriages. A few years ago I read Steven Covey's book *The 7 Habits of Highly Effective People*. He explained that you could classify everything you do by whether it's important and whether it's urgent, giving you four different categories (important/not urgent, not important/urgent, etc.). I think this gives us a clue as to what strains marriages. We might know something is important, but if it's not urgent it's easy to ignore it. Maybe your husband is nervous about a presentation he has to make at work today and wants to talk (important/not urgent). Meanwhile, the telephone is ringing, and your ten-year-old son is yelling that he's out of clean underwear. Both distractions are urgent; neither is really that important in the long run, but what's going to get your attention?

If we keep ignoring things that are important but not urgent, we're going to create crises that are important *and* urgent. Maybe your spouse will threaten to separate, your kid's principal will call, or your teenager will run away. You'll spend your life putting out fires.

I think that's why so many couples split up after ten years. They haven't spent time together, and so they've forgotten why they like each other. At the same time, they throw brick after brick of misunderstanding onto the wall that comes between them, because when the other person needed them, something more urgent— though perhaps not important—came up.

To stop this dysfunctional construction project, let's remember that we're not just raising kids, we're raising families. The children, though it may feel like it, are not the most important relationship in your home. The marriage is. The quality of that relationship impacts all of the others. Unfortunately, kids are most demanding in the early years, before you've had a chance to build years of goodwill. But if you don't take time for each other in those diaper-and-spit-up days, you may not have a relationship once life settles down.

Dating your spouse, though, seems like so much effort. Not only do you need to find a babysitter, you also need to find that makeup you used to wear, hidden under the sink by the rubber duckies and Vaseline. And let's not forget the quest to find clothes that don't have mashed bananas on them. But dating, even on Valentine's Day, doesn't have to be that hard. Every now and then have a candlelit dinner after the kids go to bed. Trade babysitting with some friends so you can watch a movie. Or take the kids out in strollers so you can talk peacefully as you walk. Don't get sidetracked from what's important.

Let's see how this principle might further play out. You're snuggling with your spouse (important) when the kids burst in arguing over what TV show to watch (urgent). Time to let them hone their problem-solving skills. You're reading to your kids (important) when the phone rings (urgent). That's what answering machines are for. Some things are harder to classify, like chocolate truffles (important and urgent if I've had a bad day, important but not urgent if I'm relaxing in a bubble bath). Kisses, however, are always important. And urgent. Especially at Valentine's Day. Are you ready?

## Thanking Dad
*This column was first published June 16, 2003*

*I*t's rare that I see a movie and actually think it was money well spent, but I loved *Finding Nemo*, an animated film about a daddy fish searching for his son. My kids loved it, too, aside from the scene when a barracuda eats the mommy fish. (All over the theatre, little three-year-old voices suddenly pop up: "What happened to the mommy? Where's the mommy?") But it soon passes, and you're able to enjoy this wonderful saga of Marlin and Nemo.

Such depictions of father-son relationships are all too rare in media today. Dads, on TV and in movies, are either distant, like in *Bambi*, or bumbling idiots, like in *The Simpsons*. Our different reactions to Mother's Day and Father's Day betray this same feeling. Mother's Day is a day to pamper Mom since she works so hard all year. Father's Day is more like an affirmative action concession for men. Deep down, many feel that men just don't deserve it. Every day, after all, is father's day.

And it's not just the media. I've been in far too many conversations, I must admit, where the focus has been on how pathetic our husbands are when it comes to certain basic chores. "He went to dress the girls yesterday, and he put an orange shirt with a purple plaid skirt! I almost died when I saw her!" With all this criticism, it must be hard to be a dad. Some men, of course, may deserve it: men who are never home, men who have no relationship with their kids, or men who have left altogether. But many men, I think, do try. They just don't measure up to our expectations.

And we have expectations galore. We don't just want someone who brings home a paycheque; we want a hero, someone who is as comfortable confronting that bully's father as he is cleaning a toilet and—GASP—actually replacing the toilet paper roll. Yet men simply were not raised to be fairy-tale fathers. While women of my generation were raised to do it all—to balance being a mother with a career—most men were not. It's hard for them to suddenly become Mr. Enlightened.

The fish in *Finding Nemo* have figured out how to deal with this problem much better than we have. In the unlikely friendship between Dorrie and Marlin, neither fish lives up to the other fish's expectations.

Hopelessly optimistic Dorrie and pessimistic Marlin cause tremendous trouble for each other and drive each other crazy. And yet, in the end, both fish would rather be together than apart. They accept each others' different approaches to life.

Some women aren't too happy when their husband's "different approach" amounts to "let her do all the housework while I watch the game." And if that's where you're at, you can take steps to encourage him to do more (shameless plug: my new book, *To Love, Honor and Vacuum*, gives some tips on this). But if we're going through life trying to change our partners, they're going to feel judged and criticized. And according to John Gray, author of *Men are from Mars, Women are from Venus* (and probably a better marriage counsellor than a bunch of fish are), men thrive on appreciation and retreat when they're criticized. So judging them isn't going to help anyway!

Most men may never be as good with the kids as most women are. But kids with dads at home, even dads who don't coach soccer, are more likely to finish school and less likely to get involved in drugs or crime, commit suicide, or a whole host of other bad things. So let's show men some appreciation this week for being dads. The media sure won't, and they don't get it in very many other places. And in the end, even if the kids' clothes don't match, it's so much easier to parent with someone else than to try to do it alone, as my mother, and other single parents, will attest. For those who are fortunate enough to have a partner in the parenting process, let's encourage that relationship and be grateful it's there. The kids certainly are.

# Fathers Are Different

*This column was first published June 21, 2004*

One of women's favourite hobbies is making fun of how inept men are. I know far too often I do. When the kids were younger, my husband was completely incapable of choosing clothes for the girls to wear that didn't clash. He had this rule—that buttons always go in the back—that often made our kids look like they were walking backwards. When we were out together, with the girls wearing one of his ensembles, I felt like wearing a big button saying "I wasn't the one who dressed my kids this morning."

Keith, though, could tell similar stories about me, though they probably involve keeping the van clean rather than dressing kids. We have different strengths, and with Father's Day just passed I thought it may be useful to revisit what women expect in a dad. In short, I think we expect a mom. We want men to be just as capable of doing everything we deem important as we are, and in so doing we can undermine their relationships with the kids.

Some men, of course, have no relationship left to undermine. For too many families yesterday was a day of mourning for what they do not have: a dad who loves them. Even some families with a father who lives in the house nevertheless miss out on Dad because he's preoccupied. For those families, I can only say I understand how you feel, having grown up with a dad who took little interest in my life. Take comfort in the fact that your children can overcome this and form great relationships themselves. For those of us who do have active dads, though, let's make sure we spend the rest of the year appreciating them for what they are: not women.

When Rebecca came home from the hospital, I would snuggle with her for hours. Keith, on the other hand, liked to vigorously bounce her up and down. Had he not been a doctor, I would have demanded that he give my baby back. But Rebecca seemed to like it, and the first time she ever laughed was when Keith was doing something with her that caused my heart to stop.

Moms and dads tend to approach parenting differently. When women go out, we pack approximately 82.5 pounds worth of stuff per child, including three extra sets of clothes, sun hats, enough food for an army, a booster seat, a potty, and probably the kitchen sink. If we're lucky, men grab an extra diaper. But the kids make do anyway. That's part of the fun of being with Dad.

And dads are different. Think of the difference between the words *fathering* and *mothering*. To "father" a child takes 20 minutes, give or take a few. To "mother" takes a lifetime. Many dads, thankfully, are "parenting," but we should not expect them to mother. Indeed, psychologist David Popenoe has shown that fathers and mothers contribute differently to children's development. Moms tend to nurture and provide a safe environment to learn, while dads encourage goal-setting and independence. Kids do best with both.

Sometimes we women forget that. We'd like dads to nurture, too. Picking up a mop occasionally wouldn't hurt, either. Leaving kids with Dad too often seems like a hassle, because he does things "wrong." We go out shopping and return to a house that looks like a tornado hit. We women can manage to look after kids and clean up at the same time, so why can't they? It's not a gene defect, though. It's likely because they haven't had the practice. You can try to help him master this skill, but even if he doesn't, don't deprive your children of one-on-one time with him because it means more work for you. Kids who have good relationships with their dads have higher self-esteem, do better in school, and do better in life. That's worth a lot, even if your floor isn't always mopped.

My husband may never learn juvenile-fashion sense, but he can teach the girls to use matches and start a campfire while I'm worrying in the background about stray sparks, just as he'll likely be the one to teach our girls to drive. He's not like me. That makes life frustrating at times, but it also makes it more interesting and far more fun. Even if I do have to try harder to keep the van clean.

## Pet Peeves

*This column was first published November 4, 2002*

*This column doesn't really fit in this chapter, but it goes with the one right after. So I thought I'd put them together to help the flow.*

One of the big disappointments in my life is that an actual lizard resides at my house. I am not exactly the type of person who would willingly welcome a reptile to share my dwelling, but alas, I was outvoted by the other three members of my family, a process that makes one think democracy is highly overrated.

We could not buy a cute little puppy or a fluffy kitten because that would have required turfing out my husband Keith, who is allergic to anything with hair follicles. I let my daughters decide Keith's fate. They wisely chose to keep him, so now we are the proud owners of a hairless beast named Spotty.

Now, Spotty wouldn't be so bad if it was just *him*. I have to admit he kind of grows on you. The problem comes because Spotty, though I have tried to persuade him otherwise, actually eats like a lizard. And that means crickets. LIVE crickets.

**For many kids, pets are windows into life's messy realities.**

My husband has the revolting ability to actually grab these insects in his hand and toss them in the cage. I have evolved past that stage to the "try to trap them in a plastic bag, close your eyes, whimper and hope for the best" method. Naturally, this does not always work. About a week after we got Spotty, one escaped. I screamed. The girls screamed. We leapt onto chairs. I yelled for Katie to grab some shoes to I could swat the thing when it emerged from the closet. So there the three of us were, Rebecca shining the flashlight, me armed with two sandals ready to finish the little bugger off, and Katie simply screaming. Keith now does all the feeding.

We bought Spotty, of course, because every child should have a pet. I have not completely figured out why, because it seems to me that usually the parents end up taking most of the responsibility for feeding and walking them. But nevertheless, "kids need pets" seems to be a mantra in our society.

For many kids, pets are windows into life's messy realities. Many children's first encounter with the Grim

Reaper is burying a goldfish in a shoebox. Sometimes such lessons come too vividly. One friend of mine once had her cat spayed, only to have the animal react badly to the anaesthetic. So there the vet was, ventilating this cat (I didn't even know they DID that), until the poor creature came back to life. The grateful family brought the cat home, only to have the mother promptly back over it down the driveway the next day.

Though death may be a lesson we only reluctantly teach our kids, many parents deliberately teach their kids about birth. My friend Barb has a beautiful Sheltie named Shadow. Before getting Shadow fixed, the family decided to try to mate her. They soon found, however, that this is one of those things that sounds perfectly reasonable in theory but can be awfully messy in practice. Shadow, you see, is a rather large female dog. All the friends' dogs that Barb chose to mate her with were, shall we say, much smaller. They would put the two dogs in the garage, and the poor little boy dog, eager as he was, just couldn't reach. They eventually had to build him a ramp. The kids, though, did have the delight of witnessing the adorable puppies being born (though Barb made sure they didn't similarly witness the conception).

My children have decided that they, too, would like to witness some babies being born, and therefore they have decided that we should mate Spotty. Because of the nature of democracy and the fact that my husband thinks this would be very educational for our home-schooled offspring, I seem to be outvoted once again.

If Spotty could register a vote, I think he'd be right in there with my daughters. Lately he's been wandering around the cage looking for something—and it's not crickets, if you know what I mean. So pretty soon I may be blessed with baby Spotties, and baby crickets to go right along with them. I always knew motherhood would require stomaching some gross things, but I thought that phase passed after diapers. I was obviously very mistaken.


## Lizard Instincts

*This column was first published November 1, 2004*

think my lizard is gay. Either that or he's extremely stupid. We bought him a few years ago as a birthday present for my daughter, and as my luck would have it, my girls decided it would be fun to have baby Spotties. Once he reached sexual maturity (don't even ask how we figured that out), we dutifully borrowed a female leopard gecko from a friend and put them in the same cage.

It was then that Spotty's lack of normal lizard instincts became apparent. Lizards don't have much of a brain, but there's two things they're supposed to be able to do: catch live crickets and mate. He seemed more interested in hiding. In desperation we consulted a lizard specialist (yes, there is such a thing) who suggested that we borrow another male gecko and put him in the cage, too. If Spotty felt the competition, he would perform. That wasn't exactly the lesson on reproduction I wanted to teach my daughters, so we just told them that the lizards weren't in love and left it at that.

It occurred to me afterwards, though, that our society increasingly treats sex as if we're lizards. The wonderful thing about human beings is that sexual intimacy takes place within relationship. For women, especially, that feeling of closeness is necessary before anything else is attempted. It's one of the things that separates us from the animal kingdom: the fact that sex is not purely instinctual but imbued with relational and spiritual components.

Yet on the covers of *Cosmopolitan*, on reality TV shows, and all over the media, women are depicted trying to attract men, with most of their thoughts going towards biceps and other physical traits rather than character or personality. Pornography, of course, takes this to the extreme, but it's all part of the same continuum. When this is how we frame sex, though, sex becomes something purely physical rather than relational. We lose out on all the wonder that it can embody. And when our kids get this message, even if it's inadvertently, it's even more dangerous.

When you were young, if you wanted to have a glimpse of pornography you had to find your dad's—or your friend's dad's—stash of *Playboys*. That's not the case any more. You just need to know how to use a computer or rent a video. However, to put it mildly, it is not good for a young teen to have his or her first experience with sexuality to be pornographic. It can be very, very harmful. When kids are exposed to pornography at the same time as they are just starting to experience sexual feelings, they're going to associate those feelings with pornography rather than with a relationship. They actually can wire their brains to think of the paper image or the computer screen, rather than relationship, as sexy, making it more difficult to become attracted later on to their chosen life partner. Relationship isn't sexy; anonymous stuff is.

As parents, then, we need to keep control of the computer, especially in children's vulnerable years in their early teens. Put it in the kitchen rather than a bedroom. Install parental-control software. And, perhaps most importantly, be careful where your children hang out. Make your house the preferred hangout by providing lots of snacks and fun, or your kids may gravitate to someone else's house where the computer is far more accessible.

Finally, let's make sure we, too, don't rewire our brains inappropriately. One of the best things in life is feeling that closeness to one's spouse that derives from true intimacy. If we need to distance ourselves mentally to feel sexy, then it's as if we're not interested in our spouse but just in a body. The whole relationship is threatened, because it's clear we're more interested in a paper image than in the person we're supposed to love. That kind of rejection can devastate a relationship.

The sexual revolution was supposed to free us by allowing us to explore. I think it actually made us go backwards. Don't throw something precious away with pornography. Love your spouse, the one relationship where you can be yourself, make mistakes, and have years and years to work on intimacy. Don't be a lizard. The crickets are gross, and the sex isn't much better.

*I really wrote this column for the sake of the first sentence. I don't think anyone has ever begun a column like that, and I just had to try.*

*I also wrote it to launch my book* Honey, I Don't Have a Headache Tonight: Help for women who want to feel more in the mood, *which has a section on the danger pornography can cause in the marriage. I received some e-mails asking me to write about it, too, so I thought it was a timely subject. How sad, really.*

# The Monologues
*This column was first published March 15, 2004*

*I*f you were at the Empire Theatre last Friday, you watched women "liberating" their sexual organs as they performed the Vagina Monologues. One of the central theses of the play is that women have been silenced and taught to be ashamed of their vaginas, and we need instead to embrace them.

As the mother of two daughters, I have an awesome responsibility to help my girls develop a healthy sexuality. In my search for how to best instill these values, I came across this play. And let me tell you: this ain't the way.

First, the monologues encourage women to celebrate their sex organs in a vacuum. They are told of the wonders of masturbation and the beauty of what we used to call "private parts." But our sexuality does not exist in a vacuum. It's best expressed in relationship. The Chicago Health and Social Life Survey, echoing many others, found that the women who are the most sexually responsive are not those up on the latest S&M or bisexual techniques, or those who can yell slang words for sex organs at the top of their lungs. Instead, they're conservative Protestant and Catholic women who are highly committed to their marriages. This shouldn't surprise us, because sex is not just what's down below; it's also what's up above. When we feel safe in a relationship, we're more able to let go sexually. Yet the few men referred to in the play are primarily rapists, bullies, or perverts. Men may be the biggest threats to us sexually, but they're also our biggest allies. Focusing solely on one half of the equation fails to deal with the complexity—and the potential—of the relationships most of us yearn for.

That's not even the weirdest part. The monologues are usually performed in conjunction with sexual assault centres, with the aim of reducing violence against women. But in the play, an actress talks about being seduced by a 24-year-old woman when she was 16. Is she traumatized by the assault? No, she's happy, because she realizes "now I never need to rely on a man." Get it? Lesbian statutory rape isn't violence.

The interesting part of this scene is that in the original play, performed in the 1990s, the girl wasn't 16, she was 13. And she used to say, "If this is rape, it was good rape." That line was cut, and the girl's age changed, in 2001. Imagine the outcry if the play had contained a scene where a girl was grateful to her male rapist!

Yet it doesn't stop there. Even when the play deals with horrific violence, like the Bosnian rape camps, it talks primarily of the physical damage done, rather than the psychological damage. So the play does just what a rapist does: reduces women to body parts.

All this reminds me of Naomi Wolf, an author who became popular in the 1990s because she epitomized "fun" feminism. She's currently in the news because she has accused a former Yale professor of putting his hand on her thigh twenty years ago, throwing her into two decades of "spiritual discomfort." But here's how this story unfolded. As a 19-year-old, she invited her professor to her apartment at night, where she dressed provocatively, lit candles, and served him wine. Then he put his hand on her thigh; she vomited; and he left. Should he have done it? No. Is that sexual harassment? Technically yes, though I think calling it that diminishes cases when women weren't acting seductively, their jobs or academic futures really were threatened, and he didn't take no for an answer. Besides, she acted inappropriately, too.

Women want to flaunt our sexuality, but we seem to forget that men have theirs. We want men to respect us, but we don't always show them any respect in return, as the play and Ms. Wolf both demonstrate.

I know what I want to teach my girls. Don't be ashamed of your bodies, but don't idolize them, either, or use them unkindly to hurt men. Be careful of men who may hurt you, but don't reject men altogether. Instead, I pray that you will both find great husbands with whom you will have lots of fun. I can't believe that in this society, I'm almost embarrassed to admit that I want that for them.

*I was really scared about the reaction to this one but was the most pleasantly surprised of any that I've written. People from all walks of life told me they completely agreed with me. I received lots of e-mails, but this one covered everything really well:*

Was I ever glad to read your column on Monday! Since the show, I had been trying to make sense of what I had seen. Were my friend and I the only ones who questioned what we actually heard that night? When we reached the parking lot that night we looked at each other and said, "What was that?" (We actually were doubled over laughing because we were so glad that we both had the same queries!)

Sure there were a few good laughs in the show, but I came away feeling that women were actually taking steps backwards instead of forward. I have a 16-year-old daughter that I am trying to instil values in and that show in no way depicted what I would want for her. The lesbian story with the older woman and young girl came across to me like it did to you. In that story when the mother called to check on the daughter the older woman told her not to tell that anything was going on! Is that not against what we are now telling children to do when something they don't feel comfortable with is happening to them—GO TELL someone you trust. It was like a slap in the face to the Sexual Assault Centre...

I totally agree with you that a healthy attitude about sex is established in a committed relationship and that is the best thing we can show for our children...I was not offended necessarily because our generation has seen and heard a lot, I was just disappointed I guess...My friend and I were beginning to think that we were the minority—we were dying to find out what others thought (we never thought we were that conservative!). Your column helped us to work through our thoughts—this is one for us to laugh about for a long time to come!

*When you write, it really can't get much better than that. I thought something she said, though, was very telling—"my friend and I were beginning to think we were the minority." Because the media and the wider culture tend to praise things like this play, it's easy for us to feel as if there's something wrong with us if we focus on the fact that it's, well, gross. But what if we're actually the majority, but nobody's speaking up any more? We're all too scared.*

*I think we should start speaking up, whether it's about something like this or about parenting problems, or the way schools are run, or spanking, or marriage. The conventional wisdom, you see, may not actually be that wise. I don't think we are the minority. We just have to be louder so people will start thinking for themselves once again.*

# The Three R's

It's hard to write columns on schooling because my kids don't actually go to school. Or rather, they don't go to the public school. They go downstairs to our kitchen table. You see, we home-school, and as such, I probably have quite a different perspective on schooling than most parents. My oldest daughter did attend JK and SK at a public school, but we've been teaching them at home since.

We home-school because we believe we can give the kids a better education at home, we can be with them more, they can participate in more activities (like music and gymnastics) without cutting into family time, and they can grow closer as siblings. Though we love home-schooling, I know that it definitely isn't for everyone. But whether parents home-school or not, one of our biggest challenges is our children's education. When I talk to my friends, one of their primary struggles always seems to do with some aspect of school, whether it's not getting along with a teacher, a child who's struggling to learn, a child who's bored because he learns too quickly, or a child who's in with the wrong crowd.

Many of my columns, then, tend to be about school because, as a home-schooling mom, I think about education a lot, and, as a friend, I know how much children's problems in school can impact the family. I find it difficult to write these columns, though, because I know many teachers try hard and do a wonderful job with what they're given, and I don't want to discourage or insult them by any means. I still feel, however, that the situation holds a lot of room for improvement. I hope I succeed in walking that fine line between advocating for better schooling and praising those in the trenches, but you can judge for yourself as you read these thoughts.

## Why School Isn't Starbucks

*This column was first published September 9, 2002*

Backpacks litter your front hall; lunch boxes sit, with contents untouched, in the sink; and overtired children melt down just as you put dinner on the table. The school year is upon us again, and with it our renewed hopes for our children: that they will learn, that they will make friends, or, at the very least, that they will not be social misfits.

And there is no one who shares your goals more than your child's teacher.

Now, that may be hard to believe if you're still waking up in a cold sweat with images of your fifth-grade teacher—who bore a scary resemblance to Morticia of the Addams family—looming before you. If a bad experience with a teacher thirty years ago has the power to render us blithering idiots at 2 a.m., no wonder we're so defensive about our kids!

Most teachers, though, went to teachers' college to make a positive difference in children's lives, and not to learn how to destroy their spirits. They're on your side, and this year they'll have more opportunity to influence your kids positively than anyone else, next to you, will. But while your goals may be the same, your agendas certainly are not.

Picture it like this: you're looking for the mocha cappuccino grande of education, with thick, rich foam smothered in chocolate swirls. You want the individualized attention, the stellar curriculum, and the teaching tailored to your child's learning style. Your child's teacher, though, probably doesn't have a cappuccino machine. He or she has an old faithful percolator that makes black coffee—and definitely decaf at that.

Your teacher can't give your child the bells and whistles—no matter how much he or she wants to—until the class is subdued, which is no easy task. Likely there are 25 or more students in the class, all too many of whom show up to school on the first day without an adequate lunch, backpack, or snack, and with a runny nose and dirty clothes to boot.

The only way the teacher can teach this hodgepodge of kids is to figure out how to get all 25 to listen at the same time. This requires conformity, not individuality, and it can be awfully hard for some kids to adjust to. Put them in a class where twenty others are swinging their legs, picking their noses and eating it, giggling, passing notes, or making faces, all while supposedly learning long division, and they can't function. Much as the teacher may want to give each child attention, keeping these kids corralled has to come first, and it can be an exhausting task.

As a parent, you can help your child by becoming the teacher's ally in this taming of the masses. Start the year not by making demands but by offering encouragement and help. Tell the teacher about little Johnny's problems recognizing *b* versus *d*, or how sitting near a certain child will turn little Johnny into a miniature Charles Manson. Teachers cherish tidbits like these; that's one more thing they don't have to learn the hard way. Send encouraging notes, and ask in what areas your child needs extra coaching. If you can find time, go on field trips or volunteer at the school. Help do some of that corralling yourself.

But it's not just the practical help teachers cherish. My friend Adam, who teaches grade 4, says it's just comforting to be reminded that parents really do care, for all around them is evidence that too many do not.

This alone can build a sense of common purpose with the teacher. And if you can keep these lines of communication open, you can build a relationship so that, if a problem surfaces, the teacher can tell you before it gets out of hand. Otherwise, you risk being summoned in because Johnny never understood first semester's math, and now he's taking out his frustration by punching kids at recess. How much better to learn of this the first time Johnny can't complete an assignment!

So make the teacher your ally, and then, in thirty years, your kid is less likely to wake up screaming in the middle of the night. And more likely to remember long division.

# Why I Hate Dick and Jane

*This column was first published September 30, 2002*

*R*ecently, my husband and I met with some friends whose third-grade son was dreading school. Reading for him was tortuous, and so school had become a jail sentence. The teacher's solution to this seemed to be to "share the pain." He was now to read aloud to a parent for 20 minutes each night.

I don't know about you, but if I were an 8-year-old boy who already felt that I couldn't read, being asked to read out loud at home would be a nightmare, even if it were necessary. And can you imagine sitting through that as a parent? Why not simply bang your head against a wall!

Perhaps the reason we're producing such poor readers is because we take all the joy out of reading. Two years ago, my daughter was in senior kindergarten with a wonderful teacher. The school had an admirable goal of encouraging kids to read with their parents, and so launched a "book-in-a-bag" program, sending home a new book every night. But listen to the type of book they chose: "Look! The sun. Look! A bunny. Look! A turtle. Look! A cloud. Look! It's Mommy!" So kids who are struggling to read learn that reading is not only hard, but it's also mind-numbingly boring.

Of course, today's schools aren't the only ones to blame for this inane level of story telling. The Boomers grew up with the infamous Dick and Jane: "See Dick. See Jane. See Dick run. Run, Dick, run." If I had to sit through that, I'd soon be having murderous dreams: "See Dick die. Die, Dick, DIE!"

I won't go into a discussion about why these books are structured as they are, because that's a subject for a whole other column. Let me just say here that many kids have little incentive to read: it's hard, and it's no fun. Let's see how we can take the school's two ideas—to read with your kids and to help them practise reading, too—and make these actually enjoyable for everyone. Instead of banging our heads against the wall or keeping our eyes open with toothpicks, let's huddle on the couch together with a good book. If you want to raise a reader, that's the recipe. It's quite simple: *Read great books to your kids. Even when they're older.*

Too often we stop reading to them because we figure they should read to themselves now, but then we miss a wonderful opportunity to connect as a family. Do you remember your favourite books when you were young? I cried when Matthew died in *Anne of Green Gables*, laughed with Jo in *Little Women*, and rejoiced with Laura in *Little House in the Big Woods*. As I experience these adventures again with my own daughters, it's almost like meeting long-lost friends.

We suggested our friends go to the library and check out classic books to read to their son—like C.S. Lewis's *Narnia* series—and maybe some easier ones he can read himself. But some boys will always prefer the real and the gory over make-believe, so non-fiction books on killer sharks, volcanoes, or mummies may pique their interest better. Then we suggested our favourite trick: make his bedtime a firm 8:00 (it varies now between 8 and 8:30), but let him stay up until 8:45 if he's reading. What kid will say no to that? As children read more, reading becomes a natural part of life and stops being so intimidating.

Some kids develop a mental block to reading because it's so stressful at school. Sharing good books together at home and letting them read leisurely themselves takes the tension out of the activity and lets them enjoy something for which there is no substitute. Then, when you do work on reading at home, it's in the wider context of enjoying books together.

When your children fall into a book, they experience a world they may never be able to otherwise. Maybe if we introduce them to this magical world, they'll be more eager to read and less likely to think of reading—and the schooling that goes with it—as an unpleasant chore.

*My first version went like this: "See Dick die. Die, Dick, die. Die, die, DIE!" I took out the last bit for word-count reasons. But I still like it better, and it's become a mantra around our house whenever we read a book we think is really poorly written. "Die, Dick, die. Die, die, DIE!" My kids love it.*

## What's a School For?
*This column was first published November 25, 2002*

For all of you out there who hate the new standardized tests because they don't really measure your kids' successes, participants at a recent Ottawa education conference hear your pain. They don't think the tests tell the whole story, either. They don't want to abolish them, though. Instead, they want to monitor *other* areas of your kids' lives, too, to make sure schools are doing the proper job. In fact, they want to make sure the schools are doing *your* job.

These educators have decided that a true measure of the success of the school system comes from producing students who don't get pregnant and don't contract STDs; who exercise regularly and aren't obese; who grow up to vote, volunteer, stay off drugs and stay off welfare; who don't smoke and don't drink; who do graduate; and, oh yeah, who maybe know some math. To monitor whether a school is successful, then, standardized tests aren't enough. What if all our brilliant kids were fat and didn't brush their teeth?

> A school's primary function was once to teach academics. Today it's to teach attitudes and behaviours.

Today, if a study shows that something will benefit kids—even if it's standing on their heads for twenty minutes a day while whistling "On Top of Old Smokey"—we all declare, in one loud voice, "The schools have to do something about that!" We certainly can't rely on parents, the thought goes, because then kids who have neglectful parents will miss out on some vital lessons.

A school's primary function was once to teach academics. Today it's to teach attitudes and behaviours. The government is now insisting that high schoolers can't graduate unless they complete their forty hours of community service. This year, though, they've issued a waiver to allow students to don their caps and gowns even if they don't pass the grade 10 literacy test. We would rather have volunteers than workers.

Volunteering, of course, is vital to society, as are most

of these other lessons the school now teaches. But can a school really do in 6 hours a day (4 if you take out lunch and recess) what parents can't do in the other 18? The school system, no matter how well intentioned, can't make up for inadequate parenting. Take the latest push to overcome obesity. Many educators feel that we need to give kids more gym classes with more aerobics. But according to the Canadian Pediatric Society, the best way to lower obesity rates is to get kids to turn off the television and to stop eating junk food. The schools can't do this, no matter how hard they try. The parents hold the keys, as they do to so many other things.

Yet not only are we asking schools to do the impossible, we're also asking them to take valuable teaching time to do what, for many kids, is simply unnecessary. One of my friends teaches grade three, and she told me about a weekly visit they had from the Health Unit to teach kids to socialize better. As anyone who has ever set foot in an elementary school classroom knows, you can't teach 25 kids if even one child is running around the classroom banging kids' heads together, yelling, or throwing scissors (it happens). You have to address these behavioural issues first. But in this case, they took teaching time away from 24 kids who didn't need it to reach the one who did. Interestingly, the whole class wasn't forced to sit through a remedial reading lesson that may have benefited three or four, but they were asked to sit through a remedial behavioural lesson that benefited one.

Kids without proper parenting need guidance, and the schools do seem like the only solution. As a society, we certainly need them to try. But I have very little confidence that they can truly succeed in raising kids with healthy behaviours and attitudes if parents aren't onside. And in the meantime, teachers are exhausted because there's too much on their plates, and the government is frustrated because test scores are so low. And those kids who do have good parenting lose out on valuable class time while teachers tell them how to reduce STDs, avoid pregnancy, sympathize with those from other cultures, and use deodorant. I can do all those things better at home. I'd rather my kids learn to multiply. How about you?

*The day that this column came out I received about 5 phone calls around 5:30 at night from people telling me to, quick—turn on your radio! It turns out Joey Martin, the DJ from Mix 97, the most popular radio station in my hometown, was reading it on the air. That was a thrill like no other I had experienced before! I also learned later that some teachers had cut the column out and put it up in their staff room. That made me feel much better, because I didn't want to insult teachers in writing this and I was glad they didn't take it that way. The Health Unit was fairly angry at me, though. They wrote a letter to the editor saying they had never done any socialization classes. I know the third-grade teacher I mentioned well, though, and she swears that the school sent someone into her classroom to teach proper behaviour. Perhaps this person wasn't from the Health Unit (though that's what the teacher remembers), but somebody was there. I am sorry if I maligned the Health Unit, but I still think such classes—regardless of who is teaching them—are a waste of time.*

# The End of Education

*This column was first published January 13, 2003*

*I*t's January, and high school seniors are frantically filling out their university applications, with visions of being sucked up by The Double Cohort Monster haunting their dreams. While they twist themselves into knots trying to make themselves look attractive ("The many parties I attended throughout my high school years helped to improve my communication skills, taught me compassion, and inspired a love of nursing that I would now like to pursue"), I think it's worth looking at whether university is worth all the fuss.

You've scrimped and saved for years, but what are your kids going to study with your money? Well, if they're at Harvard, they can take a course called "Who is Black?" UCLA offers a "Cultural History of Rap." Other universities offer pornography as an insight into heterosexual relationships; the true message of "The Simpsons"; soap operas as an insight into the family; and my personal favourite, from Georgetown, "The Philosophy of Star Trek," which ponders such questions as "Is Data a Person?" and "Could you go back in time and kill your grandma?"

Now, these courses may inspire debate and actually be quite difficult (think of how long it would take to watch all those "Simpsons" episodes), but if we're not also requiring kids to take a survey of history, or literature, or even civilization, they have no context for it.

Of course, you may argue, the point of university isn't just to learn a set of facts; it's to be exposed to different viewpoints. Well, if that's what you're after, hold a family reunion. Your kids are more likely to encounter differing opinions debated vigorously there than they are at any university today. An American survey of university arts professors found that in 2000 89% voted for Gore, a further 9% voted for Ralph Nader, and only 2% voted for Bush, despite the fact that in the general population, Bush and Gore were almost evenly split. There's nothing wrong with voting liberal, of course, but if all professors believe the same thing, then how can real debates happen on campus?

I don't have the data for professors' political leanings in Canada, but I would suspect it is similar. Queen's offers a course called "The Sociology of Art and Culture," which is described this way: "We will be gazing at and looking for classist, sexist, and racist content in popular culture." Note that the professor does *not* say "we will look to see if biases exist," but instead says "we will gaze at...sexist and racist content." There's not even an effort to appear objective.

A student with a liberal arts education was once a catch in the job market because he or she possessed wonderful analytical and problem-solving skills. University was supposed to teach the theory, while colleges taught the application. Because of the direction universities are going, though, students not only have little application, they also lack the strong theoretical background that was once their trademark.

As parents, we have three goals: teaching kids to be independent; getting them educated; and, above all, making sure they don't move back in with us once it's all over. The latter two goals are becoming increasingly out of reach. For several years now, studies have shown that colleges give far more bang for their buck in terms of future employability. Unless your child is aiming for a profession that requires university, like medicine or law, often more practical education is found elsewhere.

I don't mean to disparage university entirely, though. University certainly can be a way up the mobility ladder. It does encourage independence, teach writing skills, and introduce kids to new ideas (probably the ones you'll hate). And it does give them that still-prestigious degree. For too many kids, though, it has become a rather efficient way to waste $40,000.

Since the universities will be overflowing next year, many students will be forced to make other choices. And when they do, and the sky doesn't fall, we may learn that they're not missing much. Maybe the emperor has no clothes. For the sake of our children, and Canada's economic future, it's time to figure out why this is so and change it for the better.

# Do Schools Fail Boys?
*This column was first published May 5, 2003*

ake a survey on whether there's sexism in schools, and almost everyone will agree there must be. Girls are discouraged from taking math and science. Girls are afraid of looking too smart. Boys are called on more often. Girls do well until they hit their teens, and then everything falls apart. News stories are full of how schools shortchange girls.

In this light, I find the following statistics puzzling. In British Columbia, 66% of incoming first year medical students are women. Sixty percent of university undergraduate degrees are awarded to women. Girls are more likely to finish high school, to go to university, to join debating clubs, and to join student government. While girls have largely closed the gap with boys in achievement in standardized tests in math and science, boys continue to lag behind girls in reading and writing, and that gap is widening.

But lest you fear that girls have the upper hand in everything, here's where boys excel: they are more likely to drop out, to do drugs, to be suspended, to be arrested, to be diagnosed with ADD or learning disabilities, and to commit suicide. It is not girls who are failing to learn; it is boys who are failing, and not just in Canada, but in the United States and Britain, too. And it is us who are failing them.

Why do schools fail boys? I'm not sure, but here are some of my theories. Imagine you're a 5-year-old boy and you're entering kindergarten. All around you are women—women teachers, women librarians, women principals—all of whom want you to sit still, line up straight, and don't play rough. You read books about turtles and aardvarks trying to work through their feelings, rather than about mummies rising from the dead or earthquakes or sharks or spaceships. Even in gym class you're not allowed to do what you want to do. You can only run when they say "go," and then you have to stop.

Then you join a hockey team. You're allowed to be rough. You're allowed to yell. Men are everywhere. And Dad comes to see you play. Where are you going to want to focus your energy? At school, which is boring, or at sports, where boys can be heroes?

Of course, not all boys like hockey and not all girls like to sit still. But my husband sees many boys in his office for behavioural problems whose only real problem is that they're too easily distracted. They're simply normal boys, who find it difficult to sit at a table with eight other kids and do seatwork while other kids are at other centres around the classroom. Girls don't have this problem to nearly the same extent.

The problem is not only learning styles, though. It's also what we're expecting kids to learn. One Brit wrote about how we're even changing our curriculum to mirror girls' concerns: "Whereas before a typical history question might have read 'give an account of the key events during the reign of Queen Victoria, and explain why they are significant,' the question now reads 'Describe what it might have been like growing up in a Manchester poorhouse during the reign of Queen Victoria.' Instead of fact-retention and recall, in which girls and boys are roughly equally proficient, the question now requires empathy, something that females excel in, and at which males are useless."

In Ontario, the Durham school board took one look at its standardized test scores and ordered all its schools to come up with action plans to address the problems boys face. While 59% of their grade 6 girls met the standard for reading, only 39% of boys did, similar to the gender discrepancies in other boards. Durham, though, is the only one so far to address this specifically.

What should these action plans involve? I don't know. I would hate to see us change schooling so that now girls were disadvantaged. But surely there must be a way that schools can be made more flexible so boys can be more engaged. What do you think? Send me your ideas, and I'll write a follow-up column.

*I did get some great e-mails on this one! A lot of people were curious as to why I care so much, since I don't have any boys. But I don't think it's good for society for either sex to be at a disadvantage. Here's what I wrote next:*

## Boys Will Be Boys
*This column was first published May 26, 2003*

used to think that all children were blank slates, with everything, from their gender identities to their personalities, still to be written. By giving them Barbie dolls or trucks I could determine who they would be. Then I actually had kids. When Rebecca was a year and a half old, I was pregnant, sick, and I couldn't have found my makeup if my life depended on it. My favourite clothes were maternity sweat pants. And yet this little girl, who had no role model for "pretty," was constantly reaching into her closet to get down her one white, frilly dress. I couldn't understand it.

My friend Barb had a similar experience. She had three boys, and then along came Annie. Annie didn't want to play with any of the boys' toys, even though the house was riddled with them. She wanted her dollhouse. The boys, to be fair, liked the dollhouse, too, but they liked it because of the neat sound effects they could make as they shot the dolls through make-believe cannons.

Boys and girls are simply different. Obviously not all boys like weapons and not all girls like dresses, but things tend to go in these directions. It seems like that blank slate isn't so blank after all. Yet in many ways, schools still function as if we can, and should, shape kids' personalities. The way schools seat students, the games they play, and the stories that they read all show that they value peace-loving, co-operative, loving, and friendly behaviour. Schools tend to emphasize teamwork, talk about feelings, and try to avoid too much competition. Many even have "student of the week" awards to reward kids who have been nice to others, rather than to reward those who have made the biggest improvement in math.

These are all very admirable qualities. But there's one serious flaw. All of these things, without exception, tend to be associated with "feminine" traits rather than "masculine" ones. (Again, I'm not saying all girls are peace loving and all boys aggressive, but the norm tends to fall in this direction.) But if we hold up feminine traits as the ideal, at some level we're telling boys they're not good enough.

Yet many masculine traits are also very useful in learning. Studies show that boys tend to value independence, competition, and success, and all students could benefit from an injection of these values. Instead of viewing these things as useful in their place, though, we're trying to teach the boys to be more like girls.

This was a common refrain in the replies I received to my column asking, "Do schools fail boys?" One mother complained that her son simply didn't learn with paper and a pencil. He's very concrete and would rather learn measurement by going outside and picking up sticks that are 5 cm, 10 cm, or 20 cm long than by drawing lines on paper with a ruler. Another mother reported that her son doesn't respond to his teacher, who is very passive. He needs someone with a firmer hand, who won't be afraid to raise his or her voice every now and then (a recent study found that many boys tried harder if they were spoken to harshly when they misbehaved). Nevertheless, as a society we've tied teachers' hands by threatening to sue if they raise their voices even a little or if they so much as touch our little darlings while these kids roam around the room making fun of kids who are actually working.

Our schools are not working for many boys. They stress teamwork and seatwork but at the same time prevent teachers from performing almost any kind of discipline other than a "time out" or a suspension (both of which many boys see as rewards, because they get excused from the very activity they were trying to avoid in the first place). Let's acknowledge that these boys need a whole different approach to learning. Our future depends on helping everyone to be the best they can be. That won't happen if we try to deny important parts of who boys are. There is no "one size fits all" approach to education, and maybe we should stop pretending there should be.

# What Your Child Won't Read This Year
*This column was first published October 6, 2003*

When you hear the word *snowman,* what do you think? If you were to read that Christopher Reeve was "confined to a wheelchair after his fall," how would you feel? If you answered "offended" (*snowman* is sexist; *confined to a wheelchair* is condescending to those with physical challenges), then have I got the job for you! You're the perfect candidate for the textbook companies that are feverishly rewriting our children's readers, social science books, and more to make sure everyone has a safe and inoffensive—albeit boring—education.

Thankfully, this isn't going unnoticed. Diane Ravitch, in her book *The Language Police*, shows in painstaking detail how political correctness has led to an abolishment of any core curriculum in the social sciences and has rendered textbooks so mind-numbingly boring that no student should be expected to read them without Ritalin. Luckily, with the increase in Ritalin prescriptions, fewer and fewer are required to. Ravitch is specifically writing about the American experience, and though I found much research about textbook revision in the States and Britain, I couldn't find the Canadian equivalent. But even if we're not as bad as they are, we're probably not far behind. So here's what our kids can soon expect.

On the U.S. national fourth-grade reading test that Clinton established, no white boys were the heroes in stories. All heroes were either female or non-white. In one passage, a white boy weeps, "If only my big sister were here, I would know what to do."

In addition, anything that anybody could find remotely offensive is removed. References to a sequoia tree branch being so big that even a seven-foot man could not reach around it were deleted because they were sexist. The bias panel also rejected a passage about a blind person who climbed Mount Everest, because it may have implied that the blind have more difficulties than those with sight do. They rejected an article about the manufacturing of peanuts, because it didn't mention that some people are allergic to peanuts. And then they deleted a story in which a rotting stump in the forest, which was inhabited by insects, mosses, birds, reptiles, and small animals, was compared to an apartment building. This could be offensive to those who live in apartments. And it's not just the Americans. On the other side of the Atlantic, school districts in England have banned any stories that focus on pigs, because it may offend some religious sensitivities.

Not only do we have to make sure we don't offend anyone, we also have to be careful not to reinforce any stereotypes. Riverside, a major textbook manufacturer, has a long list of stereotypes they are not allowed to depict: men being strong, brave or silent; women crying; boys playing sports; girls playing with dolls; men working as lawyers, doctors, or plumbers; women working as secretaries or nurses; elderly people suffering from physical deterioration; older women knitting; African Americans being athletes; women being stay-at-home moms; and so many more.

**Only the least controversial pieces make it past the censors.**

The end result is that only the least controversial pieces make it past the censors. Yet think about the great stories you loved as children. Would they pass this test? Take "Old Man and the Sea." You won't see a piece like that in textbooks, because *old* is ageist, *man* is sexist, and *sea* is discriminatory against those who live inland and may not understand what is meant. Call it "Old Person and the Medium-Sized Body of Water" and you might have a chance of getting it through. But in the meantime, say goodbye to Mark Twain, Jack London, Ernest Hemingway, John Steinbeck, Herman Melville, Louisa May Alcott, and more. If our kids do read passages by them, they're likely to be edited so that all the "bad" parts are taken out—along with all the beauty of the language in which they wrote. So don't expect your kids to know about Frosty the Snowman, the Three Little Pigs, or even Scout's dad's heroism from *To Kill a Mockingbird*. They're all too offensive, and our poor little kids can't handle it.

*A number of readers weren't sure that this was really going on in Canada. In some ways, though, I think Canada is worse. I have a series of booklets, one on every country in the world, that I picked up at a library sale, published by the University of Toronto for use in middle school. I came across several interesting "facts" when I read them. Did you know that Cuba has complete freedom of religion? It's too bad those priests and pastors in Castro's jails haven't been informed of that. And that after Israel declared independence in May 1948, a civil war broke out? I thought it generally was not called a civil war when five foreign powers invade you (in this case, Egypt, Syria, Jordan, Lebanon and Iraq). That's like calling World War II the French Civil War. We are so concerned with being multicul- turally appropriate and inoffensive that we can't tell the difference between good and evil any more. I find that very sad, and it's one of the main reasons we home-school.*

## Train Your Brain
*This column was first published April 12, 2004*

I grew up watching and loving Big Bird, but a new study in this month's *Pediatrics* magazine says that our yellow feathery friend may actually be the enemy. Each hour of television that children between the ages of 1 and 3 watch leaves them 10% more likely to develop attention problems at age 7.

Now I know this is a controversial study, since it seems to blame parents for kids' problems. I'm not a scientist, and I haven't done any studies myself, so you'll have to take my conclusions with a grain of salt. But here's what I think. ADD has been increasing, and many children who don't have full-blown ADD still have trouble paying attention. Some kids, biologically, will have ADD no matter what. I think, however, that these kids are the exception. There must be a cultural component to explain why it's becoming so prevalent now. TV seems like a good explanation.

Think about it. Big Bird dances. So does the letter *D. J*, on the other hand, jumps. It also jangles, jiggles, and jives. And it jangles for less than 10 seconds before it begins to jerk or to jog. When children watch this, they learn that nothing should ever take longer than approximately four blinks of the eye. After that, it's time to move on. They're also taught that everything should be entertaining. Letters dance and sparkle. Numbers laugh and sing. When they get to school and see a piece of paper with lots of *P*'s to trace, they wonder what's up. *P*'s not moving. So they do. Time's up.

Television may actually wire our kids' brains in the wrong direction. What if attention isn't something we're born with but something we learn as we grow, just like we have to learn to pee before we put the snowsuit on and to go to sleep in a big-girl bed without needing Mommy to lie down with us? And what if, instead of teaching it, our society is now teaching the exact opposite?

Think about life one hundred years ago. There was no television. Kids didn't even have many toys. If they wanted to play, they had to make up games. Playing was active, not passive. It involved the imagination and it engaged the brain. At the same time, kids were also disciplined much more harshly (much of which, I think, was excessive). They had to sit still at mealtimes. They had to sit perfectly still in church. Things did not always have to be fun.

Today everything involves entertaining kids. We don't even have plain old wooden blocks any more. Today's blocks whistle and sing. Kids, whose brains are still being formed at this young age, aren't actually stretching them. What a nightmare this creates for teachers! Instead of figuring out the best way to explain a complex concept, teachers have to figure out how to keep kids' attention.

Maybe it's time to get serious about wiring kids for attention. April 19–25 is this year's TV Turnoff Week, proving to millions of kids a year that it is indeed possible to tune out. We may all need special videos for emergency time to ourselves, but if that emergency time is taking 5 to 6 hours a day, there's something wrong. Instead of reaching for the remote, let's reach for a book, even when kids are under a year. Let them hold one, play with one, even bite one. Let it become their friend, so that as they grow they will be drawn to books.

What if your child is older and already has problems with attention? I've heard of people with brain injuries who overcame them by practice. They spent hours each day drilling themselves on the areas of the brain that no longer worked, to try to build different neural path-ways. I'm not a neurologist, and I'm not sure if that really works if your child has severe ADD. But for the vast majority who just have minor problems, maybe a little brain exercise will help. So turn off the television and open up a book. Or learn to recite some funny poetry. Or take music lessons. Do something that trains the brain, and maybe, in a little while, *J* won't have to be jazzy. It can just be *J* again.

*A few readers were angry with me about this column. They sent me e-mails and links to arti-cles on the Web telling me that researchers don't believe that ADD is linked to television. But my column was based on a new, very large study just done. You can't really tell me I'm wrong until you tell me why this study is wrong. Perhaps it is; I'd love to know more about the subject because we have to do something. ADD is a huge problem. Just saying "there's no truth to the link between ADD and television," though, doesn't cut it. You can't dismiss this study that easily. It was done rigorously on a large, random sample. And that's why I find it so compelling.*

## Upgrading Your Child's Capacity
*This column was first published September 13, 2004*

ast year, the Hastings and Prince Edward School Board graciously sent me a copy of their annual report, proudly announcing that local schools are "creating a capacity for excellence." What a great slogan. If kids aren't excellent, you see, that's okay. The Board never claimed they would be. They're just creating the *capacity* for excellence.

I would have preferred "Aiming for Excellence," or "Teaching for Excellence," or even "Encouraging Excellence," myself. But never fear. Boy, do these kids have capacity.

I always thought that a child's capacity was created by their parents, but it turns out I was wrong. Children are sent to school like a blank slate, and the school is the one that shapes them. This isn't exactly the model of child development I'm used to, but the board seems comfortable with it. There's only one problem, though. If they're the ones creating the capacity for excellence, then they can't turn around and say that children's potential for success depends upon parental involvement in the form of homework help, or reading aloud, or just being there. You can't have it both ways.

Perhaps I'm being unfair, because I'm sure the board did not actually mean that they were more important than parents. In all likelihood, they were looking for a catchphrase that sounded good without actually promising too much, and they locked on to this one. The scary thing is that these people run our schools, and it doesn't seem as if their grasp of English is stellar (unless they really did mean that schools should supersede parents).

Reading the rest of the annual report also leaves me uneasy. Here, for instance, is the vision statement: "To provide excellent education which prepares our students to meet global challenges in a changing world." This doesn't sound bad on the surface, and uses many popular buzzwords—*changing world, global challenges,* etc. I'd be happy, though, with a simple statement like "Ensuring each graduate can read, write, and do basic math." But that's too easily measurable. One could tell whether or not the board was meeting its goals, whereas I don't think I could prove that schools weren't preparing students to meet global challenges in a changing world. What would be my proof? It's a rather fuzzy concept.

> I'd be happy, though, with "Ensuring each graduate can read, write, and do basic math."

Again, to be fair, I'm sure the board desires that every student who graduates can read and write, but to say that straight out seems as if they're not being lofty enough and not keeping up with the times. And keeping up with the times is very big in educational circles, even though the subject matter doesn't change much. Two times two is still four. The Canadian Shield hasn't really shifted. And *i* still comes before *e* except after *c,* or when sounded as *a* as in *neighbour* and *weigh.*

We may have added computers to our curriculum, but everything else remains pretty much the same.

The educational system, though—by which I mean the bureaucrats and the academics who set policy, not the teachers—likes to come up with new terms for things, to make schools sound innovative. For instance, schools no longer teach reading and writing but "language arts," or in some schools, "communication." Kids routinely bring home "communications folders" to work on at night, but do parents know what that is? It sounds more like preparation for marriage counselling than composition practice. Bring home a writing folder, and most of us would know what to do.

Why does the education system do this? This is my home-schooling bias coming out, but I think it helps them maintain professionalism by showing that they have special knowledge that we don't. For instance, let's say your child has a marbly, purple rash that's been there since birth, and you go to see the doctor. She'll tell you he has *"cutis marmorata telangiectatic congenita,"* which is Latin for "marbly purple rash that's been there since birth." Saying it in an old, dead language makes them sound smart. I think the educational system does the same thing. In the end, though, education still comes down to teaching children to read competently, to write decently, and to do math accurately. Most kids have that capacity, but whether or not they reach it during this school year depends, in my opinion, on parents. Quite frankly, I don't think the board is aiming high enough.

*I had such fun with this column. I received the glossy brochure from the Board of Education about* six months before I wrote this column, but I felt it was better to save it for the beginning of a school year. I remember just glancing through it one night when I was bored, and then I started really laughing. My husband was trying to read, and I kept interrupting him. "You've got to hear this!" I'd say. "Do they not understand what they're saying?"

One board member—a friend of mine, and still one, I hope—told me afterwards that I had misunderstood their slogan. They weren't "creating the capacity" in children; they were creating it within the system. Maybe so, and understanding that may have changed some of the focus of what I wrote here. But I still think the phrase is a little odd. Even if their goal is to "create a capacity for excellence" in the schools, my fundamental critique still holds. Why only capacity? Why not aim for excellence in itself? It still is rather wimpy.

No matter which way you read it, though, I did try to write this so that teachers wouldn't be insulted, and I heard through the grapevine that it was up in a couple of teachers' lounges again. I'm glad, because I think teachers have a really hard job that most are doing very well. I hope one day soon they'll begin to get better support and direction from above.

# Yuletide Reflections

It's hard coming up with new things to say about Christmas. I've already written quite a few columns on the subject, so I'm not sure what I'm going to do this year. But here are my thoughts on Christmas lights, the baby Jesus, Christmas shopping, and presents. I hope they help to get you in the holiday spirit.

## I'm Making My List

*This column was first published December 2, 2002*

Salvation Army bells are jingling; snow is gently falling; kids are frantically searching through the Toys "R" Us catalogue; and motorists are grumpy. It's the Christmas shopping season, and with it comes the need to buy imaginative gifts for our close family, passable things for others, and emergency gifts to give to all those who show up at your door unexpectedly on Christmas Eve.

I actually enjoy Christmas shopping—as long as it's done the preceding January. It's shopping now that I don't like. The day of the first freak snowstorm reminded me why.

That morning, my girls and I ventured to the mall because we had awakened only to discover that someone's feet had inexplicably grown over the summer. Five minutes into our search for the perfect boot, though, the girls were explaining that I really ought to hold their coats, and their scarves, and their dolls, because they were getting hot. Then they decided to sit smack in the middle of the aisle and complain about the colours of the boots (there were no pink ones with purple polka dots). By the time we chose a pair of the blasted things, I was ready to run out screaming. Which, naturally, is why we stayed. I decided I never wanted to come shopping again, so it was best to get it all over with now. So there we were, me carrying packages, coats, and dolls, and the girls asking when we could leave. Soon I had to drag them, too, and packages began dropping like flies.

> I was ready to run out screaming. Which, naturally, is why we stayed.

At Winners I finally begged for the use of a cart. The clerk informed us, though, that we would have to return the cart to Winners itself. Not just to an outer door. Naturally, as luck would have it, we had entered the mall at the farthest point from Winners. So we pushed through the mall, my girls retrieving the packages I left scattered in my wake, until we reached the slushy outside, where we proceeded to scatter packages on the wet ground as well. Once we reached the car twenty minutes later, we trudged back to Winners.

That, however, did not complete my Christmas list. I still needed things for my beloved husband. So yesterday, minus the kids, I decided to tackle the mall once again. For these particular presents, I needed some technical advice, the kind most 11-year-old boys could easily supply. Unfortunately, none of the clerks was an 11-year-old boy, so of course they couldn't help me. I left empty-handed.

I simply hate the crowds, the parking, and the hassles. It just seems to rob the season of its beauty, its simplicity, and its joy.

Which is why I'm so grateful I've found one method of Christmas shopping that doesn't make me grumpy and does remind me of why we celebrate. It's called the "Harvest of Hope" Christmas catalogue, put out by Partners International, a Christian humanitarian organization. You buy a gift certificate for someone, and then they can choose their "gift."

For instance, they can buy a piglet for a poor family in Cambodia for $25, meals and lodging for an orphan in Nepal for a month for $20, soccer sets so kids can play on teams in Laos for $25, milk for a month for a child in Indonesia for $11, or school supplies so a child can go to school in India for a year for $10. My kids tend to rip open their toys first to see what they got and then immediately plunk themselves down with the bright catalogue and a pencil and paper, trying to figure out all the different things they can buy for $50. (The piglet is always a big hit.) Amidst all the paper and ribbons, it's a wonderful reminder of how blessed we really are. If you'd like to do something like that, phone 1-800-883-7697 for catalogues.

Much as I love this idea, though, it's not enough. I know I'll have to venture shopping again, because I do love seeing my kids' faces light up when they see their presents. But as I'm looking at the dolls, and the art supplies, and the dresses, at the back of my mind I'm always thinking, how many piglets could I buy for this...? And I sigh again. It's such a bittersweet season, isn't it?

*In early January I received a phone call from Partners International. It seems that in one week in December they had dozens of new people call them up and buy a goat. They attributed it back to this column. I was absolutely thrilled to think that I could help in that way. And the number is still good, if any of you would like to donate this year.*

## Say Cheese!
*This column was first published November 18, 2002*

hristmas is coming, which means many of us are primping hair and ruffling bows so that we can participate in that most cherished of holiday traditions: getting the family photo taken. This tradition usually unfolds as follows:

After dressing in an actual dress and styling your hair and applying your makeup, you look completely unrecognizable to anyone who knows you, since beauty products have not touched your body in any other capacity since you first went into labour. Once you are satisfied with this transformation, you coax your lovely offspring, who are busy squabbling, into their best clothes so they look spiffy, too. The baby, of course, takes this opportunity to spit up all over your dress and his new outfit, requiring several well-chosen words as you change both of you once again.

When you and the kids are finally ready to go, you frantically yell for your adoring spouse, afraid that at any minute renewed spit up or spats will wreck this picture of perfection. When he arrives, he looks exactly the same as he always does.

After waiting for 45 minutes in a room full of whiny kids and frantic parents, it is your turn on the photo table, which is covered with what closely resembles a dead polar bear. The 18-year-old photo operator, in an effort to continue with the bear theme, is wildly wagging some dilapidated teddy in front of your baby's face. This, naturally, results in him wailing and, possibly, spitting up again. By the time you're finished, you're exhausted, grumpy, and ready to trade in your family for one of the nice, smiley ones on the wall.

Like most parents, I shared this tradition for a few years. It worked well for Rebecca, my first-born and thus my "eager-to-please-so-I-can-prove-I'm-perfect" child. Though she was often rendered terrified by the teddy-bear-wagging photographer, she usually smiled on cue. She continued to smile even when we added little Katie, who decided to squirm and spit instead. Indeed, all the pictures we have of Katie taken at these studios before she's a year and a half involve her spitting. She liked it. She spit and squirmed, and Rebecca smiled.

Once she was a year and a half, Katie finally decided that the wagging-fur thing was worth a smile. In fact, she was so enthused by it that she decided it was worth a jump, too, so we couldn't get a focused picture because she was going up and down, up and down.

Then and there, I made the decision that no sane person should have to go through this charade. Besides, candid photos are so much better, I reasoned, so from now on, we would just take our favourite candid photos and blow them up for our portraits.

Such a decision sounds very lofty and mature. It is, however, entirely impractical if you have more than one child. As anyone with more than one child knows, there simply aren't any candid photos of this second child (let alone the third or the fourth). Showing your photo album sounds something like this: "Here's Rebecca's first smile. Here's Rebecca's first giggle. Here's Rebecca's first solid poop. Here's Rebecca's first step."

"Where's Katie?"

"Ummm, let me see, I must have one of her here somewhere. Oh, here she is on this tricycle. She must be, what, two or three?"

"And who's that in the foreground?"

"Oh, that's Rebecca."

My uncle, who is one of quite a large clan, once remarked to me that the first child in a family inevitably has 4,000 pictures taken of him or her within one hour of leaving the womb. In contrast, if the fourth-born has more than twelve pictures taken of him or her by the time he or she is 16, half of them are in a file at the police station.

Today, Katie no longer spits (though we're still working on the nose-picking thing), and she's getting quite good at sitting still. I'm getting my hair cut this week, so I'm ready to be totally unrecognizable, and Rebecca enjoys sitting nicely, if only to prove she can do so better than her little sister. So before the Christmas rush is over, we shall venture down once more to get a new family portrait. Then, when Katie is all grown up,

I'll be able to prove that, yes, indeed, she was actually a part of our family, after all.

## O Christmas Tree

*This column was first published December 23, 2002*

When I was in Canadian Tire a while ago I saw an absolutely stunning Christmas tree. It was decorated in silver bows and balls with purple accents. It was my ideal tree.

Such a tree, however, will never grace my living room. No matter how much I want a purple-and-silver one, I have too many other decorations that render a consistent colour scheme impossible. I have a family Christmas tree.

First comes the gold heart embossed with "Keith and Sheila, 1991" that we received at our wedding. Then there are all the Christmas decorations we made as children that our parents thoughtfully gave us our first Christmas together (were they trying to get rid of them, I wonder?). There's the canvas stitched candy cane Keith made, and the decorated styrofoam balls I did. Other decorations full of childhood memories hang beside them, like the angel candle holders that were on my "Baby Jesus Birthday Cake" when I was six.

And now, of course, we have added our children's decorations. At first they were fairly innocuous ones, like "Baby's First Christmas." They have since become more ambitious. One year the girls and I made dough Christmas shapes and then glued little pictures to them. Katie, who is living proof that you can survive your second year of life eating only dried playdough (believe me, it wasn't my choice), actually left nibble marks in some as she tried to eat them, too, despite the salt content. Add the decorations the girls make at Sunday school out of little paper doilies, and there's no room for those classy purple balls.

Our lives are very much like these Christmas trees. We spend so much effort trying to have the perfectly decorated life, with the right kids, the right jobs, and the right promotions. But it can be exhausting to live that way. Our work is never done. We're always on the go, and when we do sit down it's only to plan how to drive our kids to more lessons, run some more errands, or throw on yet another load of laundry before we make dinner.

The family Christmas tree, with all its imperfections, is better because it is uniquely us. Anybody can have a perfectly purple Christmas tree. Not everyone can have the one decorated with your own white doily angels and pipe cleaner reindeer. Christmas anchors us and reminds us of whose we are and of what's important. A sign at Majestic Dry Cleaners recently read "If you don't know where you're going, any road will get you there." Many of us are stuck on some side road of endless errands and work because we need a road map to get us home, a map that can only come by slowing down and reflecting, if just for a little while. With the busyness of life, we often ignore our spiritual side, never taking time to think about life, death, parenting, or our purpose on this earth. Christmas can be our road map, a time to take stock of our lives and consider if we're heading in the right direction.

Whatever your spiritual background is, the challenge is the same: let's take the time during the holidays to honour it. At my house this week, we'll have a "Baby

Jesus Birthday Cake" (chocolate, of course) to remind us that Christmas is when the all-powerful God became as helpless as a baby so he could live among us and die for us, so we could live forever with him. I don't want that just to be my Christmas message; I want to live it through the rest of the year. But if I don't take the chance now to see whether my daily life reflects my spiritual priorities, I may not have time once the daily grind starts anew.

I will gladly take my Baby Jesus Birthday Cake angels and little dough hearts over purple balls any day. That's who I am, and who I want to be. Christmas is one of the few times of year when we can contemplate life without someone telling us to move on to the next task. Let's make sure that this year we take advantage of the opportunity.

Merry Christmas, everybody!


## Yuletide Musings

*This column was first published December 1, 2003*

When I was in kindergarten, I did something so bad we almost had to leave town. I informed every single one of my classmates that their belief in the existence of a certain jolly red elf may be misplaced. For days afterwards my mother received hate phone calls from irate parents, certain that I had ruined their children's Christmases forever.

I always was suspicious of Santa. How could he be in more than one mall at the same time? But perhaps more profoundly, how come Santa ignored some kids? That year, my mother and I sorted through all my toys to find some to give to the Vietnamese refugees our church sponsored, kids who would otherwise have little for Christmas. Even though I was reluctant, she won me over by describing the lives these kids had just escaped. I couldn't help but wonder, though, how could Santa overlook these kids but still leave gifts for all the "bad boys" in my class?

> **How could Santa over-look these kids but still leave gifts for all the "bad boys" in my class?**

I don't think there's anything wrong with including Santa in your Christmas. Even my daughters think the approximately 1,316 Santas in my mother-in-law's house, including the one that dances a mean twist, are great fun. But they're not expecting him to come through for them Christmas Eve. I don't think this makes me a Scrooge. I do love Christmas. I love seeing my whole family together. I love choosing gifts. And we really enjoy making things for Nana and Grandma, and even for Grandpa (if anyone has a pattern for a Detroit Red Wings doily my daughter can crochet, can you e-mail it to me?). We have a wonderful Christmas. It's just that Santa, aside from the cool dance moves, isn't a big part of it.

It all comes down to this: I'm worried that my kids are going to get too wrapped up in presents and not enough in generosity. Whenever I hear of horrors in the news, I wonder why we have been so blessed to live in a country free of persecution, free of mass graves, free of abject poverty. With that blessing comes responsibility, and I desperately want to pass on that value to my girls. Unfortunately, that can be hard when Christmas becomes too much about the presents.

When Rebecca was almost three we had our last encounter with true Christmas innocence. As the family gathered around the tree, Grandpa handed her a gift. She was thrilled. And then Grandpa tried to give her another package. Looking confused, she protested, "But I already have a present." She didn't know more were coming, and she was grateful for what she had.

That was then. This is now. Katie never experienced that innocence because she had a big sister telling her about the haul they were about to get.

I'm determined to fight this attitude. On December 7, between 4:45 and 5:00 p.m., the Food Train is stopping at the South Church Street tracks. It's been travelling across Canada, picking up tons of food for local food banks, and entertaining along the way. Let's go with our kids and bring some food. After you do that, go through your kids' toys with them, taking those they don't play with—no matter how good—and giving them to the Salvation Army, so that parents who don't have much money can pick something up to go under the tree.

Finally, if you want to think globally, try the Harvest of Hope catalogue by Partners International that I mentioned last year. Give your kids some money and let them choose "gifts" for others. They can give a piglet to a poor Cambodian family for $25, send a child in Nepal to school for $20, or buy fortified milk for a Senegalese child for $11. You can find out more at 1-800-883-7697.

Christmas provides a perfect time to teach important lessons. Long ago I learned not to question children's beliefs in genial Red Guys, and I have passed on this lesson to my girls, so that we may all enjoy a peaceful residence in Belleville for years to come. But that's not the only Christmas lesson I want to pass on. I still recall the faces of the Vietnamese girls when they opened my boxes. That memory has stayed with me more than all the Barbies and toys I ever received. I hope I can give my girls that same kind of memory.

## Planning Christmas Dinner
*This column was first published December 15, 2003*

*It makes a lot more sense if you read it after "Saving Dinner" and "Anger is not like Flatulence" (pages 75 and 45). Enjoy.*

Can e-mail bring families closer together? I'll let you be the judge. Here is a synopsis of messages my extended family sent over an 18-hour period.

**Aunt 1:** Would you all like to come to Christmas dinner here?

**Mother, Cousin 1, Cousin 2:** Sure!

**Aunt 2:** I want to be anywhere but here, because all my cutlery and kitchen stuff is in boxes.

**Me:** Ummm, okay, but Keith's on call and he may be a little worried about being more than 15 minutes from the hospital.

**Aunt 2:** Perhaps Keith should become a helicopter pilot so he can get there quicker?

**Uncle:** If he were to fly the Canadian copters, he may crash and end up in Emerg in an ambulance. But hey, that's where he was heading in the first place!

**Uncle again:** With the first snowfall today, a great idea came to me. Wouldn't it be wonderful to have a Christmas BBQ down by the shore! We could build a big fire to thaw out our food as well as anyone who happened to wander off into a snowdrift. With all the doctors on site, I'm sure we could keep fatalities to an absolute minimum.

**Aunt 1:** Ha ha ha ha. My husband is very funny. But we will be eating indoors.

**Mother:** You know, if Aunt 2 brought all her boxes of kitchen stuff, eating by the lake would be easier.

**Aunt 2:** Perfect! Down by the lake it is. I have some new hypothermia techniques I've been wanting to try out anyway. Perhaps we can invest in an ice boat for Keith.

**Mother:** I have visions of Keith flying down the Bay, fork in one hand and slightly frozen turkey in the other. Not sure from this distance whether the fork is one of Aunt 2's or Aunt 1's. Wouldn't want him going off with the wrong cutlery. Especially after Sheila's efforts to teach the girls some table manners. If it is turkey, he should be using the dinner fork.

**Me:** Given my children's table manners and flatulent ability, I, too, am inclined to go with turkey-on-a-spit. I can assure you, though, that they will likely forget to use their forks. In fact, I'm likely to forget to come altogether. This week alone, I forgot their piano lessons, forgot Becca's dance lessons, and was so mortified I determined not to forget Katie's ballet lessons. I bundled her up, arrived at my meeting, and told everyone I had to leave at 10:52 to make it to ballet for 11. And I did make it to ballet at 11. Except that ballet started at 10. So yes, we can come. But please be grateful that even if my girls use the wrong fork, that they are at least using one; everyone should bring nose plugs; and someone will have to phone to remind me it is Christmas.

**Uncle:** Wonderful! Turkey-on-a-spit it is. Nobody

bring metal forks, though. They have a habit of sticking to the tongue.

**Cousin 2:** We seem to have forgotten a compromise. If we all build an igloo around a fire, we can be both inside and outside at the same time!

**Cousin 1:** This is what I understand. **When:** Christmas Day, time yet to be determined but hopefully the weather will co-operate and it will coincide with an ice storm or arctic gale. **Who:** Anyone who can make it whether they are playing hooky from the hospital or not; children may or not be present but do not be surprised if they show up in ballet tutus expecting a piano lesson. **What to Bring:** Many layers of clothing. I recommend a windproof layer on the outside to keep the outside wind out and one's inside wind in (very good for heating purposes). Will pack a can of beans for snacking on the drive out. In terms of cutlery contributions, I understand forks are not deemed necessary by the younger crowd and thus I will not worry so much that I can only transport plastic forks on the airline.

**Uncle:** I know! We could make it into a Reality TV show! The Survivors Christmas... "Who will be the last left on the icy floes of..."

Shortly after this, Aunt 1 disconnected Uncle's Internet and we all returned to normal. But now, at least, you know where I get it from.

*These e-mails, when put together, totalled about 5,000 words. I cut them down to 700. I'll leave it to your imagination to determine how nuts my family really is. And yes, my uncle is certainly one of the craziest.*

# Crunchy Christmas Memories

*This column was first published December 22, 2003*

*I* have the Griswolds for in-laws.

If you have not seen *National Lampoon's Christmas Vacation*, you may be in the dark. But trust me, their house is not. If we start to experience brownouts, they're the ones responsible. They've got Mrs. Santa, Frosty, the Baby Jesus, the wise men, lights, stars, and, of course, Santa and all his reindeer on the roof.

My kids love Grandma and Grandpa's house. It just wouldn't be Christmas without Frosty gazing into Baby Jesus' manger. It's part of our Christmas tradition, and traditions are important. Some people get all mushy about traditions, but I don't. I like them because most traditions are either hilarious, like my in-laws' abuse of the Hydro company, or accidental, like my Christmas memories.

An only child, I loved Christmas because it brought family. I could hardly contain myself waiting for my cousins to arrive. Yet while we always had a wonderful Christmas morning, Christmas dinners were more subdued. My grandparents were both a little senile, so regular conversation didn't work very well. Instead, my grandfather tended to spend Christmas dinner reciting an episode of *Matlock*, which he thought was actually a documentary. So we children ate silently while we learned how Matlock pulled yet another trick out of his hat.

One year my mother inadvertently began another Christmas tradition. She had just purchased our first microwave, and decided to inaugurate it by cooking the potatoes. But as you know, microwaves don't cook evenly. My cousin Danielle and I were the first to discover this.

She bit into a potato, and I heard a distinctive CRUNCH. We glanced around, but everyone else was enjoying their spuds trouble-free. I don't think they even heard her. But I, sitting right next to her, managed to pull the only other semi-cooked potato out of the bowl. There we sat, CRUNCH, CRUNCH, while my grandfather arrived at the point where the bad guy was led off to jail. Today Christmas isn't Christmas without crunchy potatoes.

I think it's these shared memories, no matter how silly, that make holidays special. You're together with relatives that you don't see often, and something unexpected is bound to happen, even if it's just having to sit through a too-detailed description of someone's recent problems with regularity, if you know what I mean. That memory is enough to provide fits of giggles for at least ten years' worth of holidays.

The sacred traditions are just as important, giving us a chance to focus again on what is really important. I find the candlelit Christmas services, the Baby Jesus Birthday Cake, or just talking about both the blessings and heartaches of the past year tremendously comforting. These aren't necessarily big things, but the repetition, and the people, make them precious.

Sometimes we try too hard at Christmas, cleaning so intensely what small, sticky hands will destroy in five minutes flat, and agonizing over the perfect present for someone who really doesn't need anything. Maybe Frosty, staring into that manger, has a better perspective. The first Christmas was awfully messy, and it wasn't a big affair. But it was special because such different people came together joyously to celebrate a momentous birth.

At our Christmas table we're still celebrating, though many of the faces have changed. I have inherited a large and boisterous family on my husband's side that doesn't do Christmas small. The *Matlock* grandparents have passed away, as has a special uncle just a few years ago. He was one of the best at steering the conversation towards other TV shows, when boredom necessitated it, and he will be sorely missed when others members of my family start to go senile. My son is not here, though my daughters are. Yet all of us can still share the collective family memories as we celebrate together.

This year I'm too busy to try too hard, so I'm going to take my own advice and just enjoy a few quiet minutes to remember a baby, drink lots of hot chocolate, cuddle my kids, and test the potatoes.

I wish you all a very Merry Christmas, too.

*My in-laws are not certain I characterized them correctly in this column. It seems that some of their friends are even worse. One might think this would be an insult, but they wear it as a badge of pride.*

## Post Christmas Confessions
*This column was first published December 30, 2002*

Christmas was over five days ago, and if you're like most families, wrapping paper and ribbon are not the only things in your garbage. A few toys will be stuffed there, too, deliberately tossed at an opportune time when your child wouldn't notice.

Christmas is a time for giving. But it's also a time that grandparents, childless relatives, and other people inflict punishment on you by giving your children insufferably obnoxious toys.

When my kids were really little, my mother-in-law gave them a doll that cried when you shook it. But it didn't just cry, it wailed like a tone-deaf banshee. It sounded like Roseanne Arnold butchering "The Star Spangled Banner." My children, of course, adored this doll. My mother-in-law loved it as well, I think partly because of the look on my husband's face whenever this pink-clad battery-powered bundle let out a screech.

**People inflict punishment on you by giving your children insufferably obnoxious toys.**

Before we moved to Belleville, I gave this prize to Goodwill, where another set of unsuspecting parents could take it home to their children. But I never confessed to my mother-in-law. Or to my daughters. Consequently, over the last four years my girls have periodically been quizzed by Grandma about the whereabouts of said doll. They have looked genuinely puzzled and turned to me for an answer. I have mumbled something inaudible and left the room.

So, in the spirit of starting this new year with a clean slate, I would like to tell my mother-in-law that I gave it away. I did not do so in my own power; Keith agreed. But it's gone. Please stop asking about it. (We love you, Mom!)

There are, of course, other toys that I wish could be donated as easily. Chief among these would be the

Dancing Santa and the Singing Frosty the Snowman. These gems—given to us, naturally, by my mother-in-law—are Katie's favourite Christmas decorations. Christmas wouldn't be Christmas if she couldn't boogie along with Santa to "You Better Watch Out." But there are times when I would dearly love to send Santa flying back home at a very high velocity.

While I have not had the guts to discard these gems, others have joined the wailing doll in the Goodwill heap. The Polly Pocket doll sets, which left very interestingly shaped wedges in the soft part of your foot whenever you stepped on them, were the first to go.

Then there was the puppet theatre that looked so sturdy at IKEA but rapidly fell apart at home, showing that Swedish common sense does not extend to children's toys, or they wouldn't make them out of cardboard.

My aunt and uncle, who do not have children, have continued this tradition of ridiculous Christmas presents, though thankfully not with my kids. Once my uncle was given one of those "laugh in a bag" toys, which you shake to produce a diabolical cackle. Naturally, he felt his young nephew would appreciate this gem far more than he would, so he passed it along at Christmas. His sister did not speak to him for six months.

However, he, too, has also been the recipient of some truly silly presents. When my grandmother was first showing signs of senility, she sent some rather odd presents to them. This uncle was given a shirt that fit him beautifully; it was well pressed, hung perfectly, and looked great. If you were a cartoon character, that is. It was bright red with white polka dots. He took a picture of himself in it next to my aunt, who was donning her own Christmas creation: a hand-knit dress that was beautiful, save for the inner-tube-like waist that looked as if it were there to cover a generous roll of fat that my aunt did not possess. So the roly-poly polka-dot couple donated their items to Goodwill, too.

I love Goodwill normally. In Toronto we lived quite near a large one, and I had a blast hunting for treasures. I still have several formal dresses I found (though where I'll wear them I'll never know), along with lots of great outfits for the kids. But I'd stay away just after Christmas, unless you're looking for loud toys or loud shirts. You never know what you'll walk out with.

*Note to self: if you want to stay in your mother-in-law's good books, it is generally good to avoid insulting her in the local paper. Must try to remember for next year.*

# *The Big Picture*

Sometimes parenting debates don't just centre on what we do as parents, but on what is going on around us, in the culture, in the government, in the media. These columns step outside of our kitchens and into the wider society. As a political junkie, as well, these are often the ones I feel most passionate about.

## Why Monet Didn't Paint Hairy Bums

*This column was first published July 7, 2003*

Call me crazy, but I don't think a picture of a hairy bum is art. If you're wondering how I came to such a profound conclusion, allow me to tell you about my family's recent visit to the National Gallery in Ottawa, where many of our tax dollars are eagerly spent. We went in with one assignment: to decide what is my children's favourite piece of art. I didn't insist they stare at every painting, simply that they walked through the rooms and at the end they tell me what they liked best.

We breezed through the "old" art—the 15th and 16th centuries, full of beheadings and haloes and other scenes that didn't impress them. They liked some of the portraits from the next few centuries, especially if the artists chose to include a puppy or a kitten.

But when we reached the nineteenth century, with the Claude Monets, the Van Goghs, the Group of Seven, and the other Impressionists, Rebecca stopped dead in her tracks. She couldn't believe how beautiful the water lily paintings were. This was incredible. This was art.

Her intakes of breath as she saw beauty, though, were rapidly replaced with shrieks of incredulity when we reached the more modern section. "But, Mommy, it's just three lines! It's three straight lines!" The guard in this particular room was kind enough to point out that said painting, consisting of three stripes about twenty feet high, if I remember correctly, cost you and me and every other Canadian $1.2 million collectively.

> It was Ugly Naked Bum at its worst. It was not pretty. And it was definitely not art.

But these shrieks were nothing compared to what emanated from their mouths when we reached the alternative art. Instead of laughs, I heard gasps. "Katie, look! It's an ugly hairy bum!" And she was right. It wasn't just a picture of a bum a la Renoir, with the curves in all the right places. This one was enough to make small children scream in horror. It was Ugly Naked Bum at its worst. It was not pretty. And to the girls, it was definitely not art.

Perhaps it was an impressive piece of photography. As someone who purchased a digital camera so that I could erase all my pictures of headless relatives rather than pay to have them developed, I'm not the best judge. But I do know that my children were not impressed.

Is art important for children? I think it is. It fills our life with beauty and speaks to us in a way little else can. And many things can be art. A beautifully arranged garden, a sculpture, a piece of music, knitted lace, or lines of poetry can also elicit these feelings of wonder. They can define a whole generation, capture a moment, and express our feelings uniquely.

Just because art can express feelings, though, does not mean that all expressions of feelings are thus art. I can put a crucifix in urine (an art exhibit paid for by U.S. government funds), but is this art? I think it's political expression. Another piece of so-called "art" that recently won a prize in Britain was an empty room where the lights switched on and off randomly. Some may think this is deep. I can think of other words for it. Then, of course, there was the picture painted by a four-year-old and submitted as a joke by his mother that won an honourable mention (they thought an adult did it). I'm not sure if the latter is actually an urban legend or not, but in some ways that's beside the point. Most of us would not be surprised about such a thing, because that's how bad much of modern art has become.

Throughout history, art has been used to inspire. Art shows us what is possible and helps us imagine new heights. Art inspires kids to study and to practise so that they can do their best, too. But when adults so distort art, there is a danger that art loses its good name, and kids—our next generation—will lose out on the wonder that art can produce. Beauty is a rare commodity in modern society. Let's not snuff it all out by calling the outrageous art. My daughter still loves Monet. She doesn't want to see a hairy bum. And frankly, neither do I.

## Spare the Rod?

*This column originally appeared October 21, 2002*

et me state the obvious first: it's generally not a good idea to spank your child with an electrical cord. That may seem like a no-brainer, but to a Mennonite family in Aylmer, using an electrical cord, or a belt, or a stick was preferable to spanking their children with their hands, because hands were to be reserved for affection. Yet spanking your child with an object can do serious damage. My husband, a pediatrician, counsels parents to avoid spanking altogether, simply because too many people do it out of anger and harm the child.

But let's give our heads a collective shake and agree that while spanking with a rod may be harmful, it certainly isn't as harmful as wrenching a six-year-old girl from her father's arms, as the Children's Aid Society did in the Aylmer case. Unfortunately, Judge Eleanor Schnall disagrees with such common-sense wisdom, and last week opened the doors for similar cases across the province by ruling that the Children's Aid worker acted correctly by removing the children from their home.

If spanking with a rod in and of itself really were horrible enough to warrant removal from a family, then my husband should have been taken away from his parents, my mother should have been taken away from hers, and likely every person you know over the age of

35 should all have been placed in goverment orphanages rather than being subjected to their horrible parents.

Yet were these parents truly horrible? My mother-in-law devoted herself to her boys, making sure they did well in school, acted appropriately, and had plenty of fun memories. My father-in-law taught them responsibility, a good work ethic, humour, and a love for the Detroit Red Wings. (The latter, much to his chagrin, didn't stick.) And yes, occasionally, they both spanked their kids with "rods," as did every other parent they knew at the time. While some Leafs fans may disagree, it's quite evident to me that the boys were lucky to have the loving parents they did.

As I've been thinking about this case, I wonder if we're misplacing our emphasis. Does spanking really rank up there as one of the worst things you can do to a child? I think it's getting all the attention it does because it's easily quantifiable: you either did it or you didn't. Because it's easy to measure, it's theoretically easy to remove children from parents who do discipline in this way. Most "bad" parents, though, will never have their children taken away, because what they do, though far worse, cannot be measured.

This family in Aylmer, by all accounts, played with their children, supervised their education, read to them, played sports with them, went strawberry picking with them, sang with them, and in general did everything they could to create a loving family environment.

On the other side of the spectrum are parents who would never dream of spanking yet would also never dream of sacrificing a Saturday afternoon to practise baseball with a struggling Little Leaguer. They ensure their children are dressed well, fed well, and have a decent place to live, but they spend almost *no* time with them. One recent study found that parents, on average, read to their children for four minutes a day. If you're reading *Goldilocks and the Three Bears*, that's not even enough time to get to the baby bear's chair!

As parents, we all crave time to ourselves. Kids, too, need the opportunity to explore, imagine, and play on their own. Too many kids, though, live lives almost completely cut off from their parents, as they watch TV in their own rooms, play Nintendo alone, and then go hang out with friends down the street. Parents may not spank, but they don't do a whole lot of anything else, either.

What does more harm? Spanking children, or simply ignoring them? One we can quantify; one we cannot. But deep inside, we know that what children need is attention and love. Our parents and grandparents may have disciplined too harshly, but they gave us that attention. I only hope our generation keeps the good parenting traditions, instead of throwing everything out as we reject their methods of discipline.

*Many readers told me how much they liked this column. The Children's Aid Society, however, did not. Their executive director sent a letter to the editor that was longer than my original column, complaining that I "advocated spanking with a rod" and going on to say why spanking was bad. I was rather upset at this, since I obviously do not advocate such a thing. I opened the column, in fact, saying that one should never do that. My argument, I thought, was quite clear: spanking with a rod is excessive but should not be the only criteria for removal from a loving home. There are things far worse that we never measure. Yet he chose not to bring up that argument at all. I have no problem with people disagreeing with me; I just wish they would actually engage in the debate, rather than mischaracterizing it. So I wrote this next one to further clarify.*

## Sheila Unveiled

*This column originally appeared December 9, 2002*

*I* had a horrid week two weeks ago. I lost my voice and felt like a truck had run over me, and by the end of the week I wished it had. Different committees I'm involved in were in the midst of pointless political squabbles. I spent the week on the phone trying to sort things out while the dust bunnies in my house grew bigger. In the middle of attempting to mend all these hurt feelings, I was suddenly paralyzed by the thought that I, too, may have offended readers in this column.

Which brings me to today's topic: unveiling Sheila's true views (not that I keep them very hidden!). Most of the responses I've received about this column have been very positive. People especially liked my lizard one (can we relate better to reptiles and insects, I wonder?), and many of you sent me funny letters asking me some questions about my life. Here are my answers to the simple ones: I *have* found a mate for Spotty (though they haven't consummated that relationship yet). I *have not* had my picture taken (though my mother is breathing down my neck). I *have* done my Christmas shopping. I *have not* vacuumed my van.

Some responses, though, have been far more critical, and I'd like to clear up some misconceptions. First, contrary to popular belief, I do not beat my kids. My column "Spare the Rod" has received more angry letters than any other (mostly since the Children's Aid response). But I never said parents should spank with a rod. What I did say is that we're misplacing our emphasis. Let me explain this with a story.

A good friend of mine was seriously hurt as an infant by her parents' negligence. She spent two months a year every year in the hospital until she was sixteen, for reconstructive surgery. She was in incredible pain. Yet, when she thinks back, what still brings tears to her eyes is the fact that nobody visited her while she was in the hospital. The emotional often hurts more than the physical. So personally, I just can't get that worked up about loving families who spank. I'm much more interested in encouraging parents to spend time with their kids, no matter what the "politically correct" views on this issue are.

> The emotional often hurts more than the physical.

In fact, invariably I'll violate "politically correct" codes here, because what I want to do is stimulate discussion and thought about how we raise our kids. If we're always saying what's "politically correct," there's nothing to discuss. Just so there's no misunderstandings in the future, though, here's a bit of a "heads-up" on my views of life:

I think kids are precious. I think Happy Meal plastic toys are not. I like marriage. I don't like divorce (I'm the child of one). I love my mother. I love my in-laws. I don't give a hoot about the Detroit Red Wings (sorry, Dad). I like Veggie Tales. Barney irritates me. I have yet to meet a teacher I don't like, but I hate the school system (though I don't think that's the government's fault, either). I hate dusting. I do like crafts, though I hardly ever finish any. A dessert is not a dessert unless it contains chocolate chips. There is no better way to wake up than to have your child kiss you. TV may entertain you, but a good book read in childhood stays with you forever. The first is a Pop-Tart; the second is a decadent triple chocolate cheesecake (with chocolate swirls, of course).

I don't think teenagers should be having sex. I do think toddlers should be taught to respect their parents. I think kids spell love T-I-M-E. I love God, and I believe God loves us, too.

And finally, I think the world would be a much better place if nobody minded dust bunnies, if kids, no matter how old they were, still demanded cuddles every day, and if chocolate were found to be the best source of calcium. And I think we'd all be a lot happier if every now and then, for no apparent reason, we emptied out of our houses and had a massive street snowball fight. So there is my take on the world, love it or not. But thanks for reading, and for all your comments. I'll try my best to inspire some more!

*This was a fun column to write. But once again I received odd letters to the editor in response. One*

*Children's Aid worker claimed that all over Belleville parents would be beating their kids thinking that I approved. Regular people, though, seemed to understand what I was saying, given all the e-mail and positive vocal responses I received. But I guess I must be a glutton for punishment, because I tried it again.*

## Spanking: Here We Go Again!

*This column was first published January 26, 2004*

ater this week the Supreme Court will rule on spanking. I'm a strange person to denounce the anti-spanking movement, since I don't spank. It's easy to abuse spanking, especially for someone like me who can be very quick-tempered. And I'm not sure spanking helps kids internalize right and wrong as well as other methods of discipline do. So I don't object to people who oppose spanking; I'm just very wary of those who work to make spanking, in and of itself, justification for government interference in your family.

Of course, those who want to outlaw spanking say they want to protect children. So far, so good. But if protecting children is utmost on their minds, then why aren't they going after the things are the most destructive?

Studies show that one of the worst things that can happen to a child is to have his or her parents divorce. This doesn't mean the child can't overcome it, but the effects are very grave. And what about something even more mundane, like growing up in a family where parents spend no time with children? Or what about children who are fed so poorly they develop adult onset diabetes when they're 10? Studies even show that childhood aggression is more linked to parental permissiveness than to any form of spanking. I'm not even sure spanking is harmful, since most studies mix spanking by a loving, calm parent in with indiscriminate hitting. They're comparing apples to oranges.

So if the anti-spanking movement isn't concerned, first and foremost, with the protection of kids, what's it trying to do? I guess it's my sociology background, but I'm drawn to the ways this movement fits in with broader parenting trends. First, spanking expresses adult authority over children, and many are simply uncomfortable with that. The best example of this came in the form of a letter my husband received that said: "We have talked to this 6-year-old boy and obtained his consent for the medical test."

Whoa. Let's back up that truck. What if he had said no? This boy was in no position to understand the ramifications of saying no. Yet we give children choice, despite the fact that they do not have the developmental ability or the life experience to understand that choice. We seem to hate exercising authority, and I think it's because authority insinuates that one person may actually know better than another, and we don't like to make those kinds of judgments.

But it's also because if we have authority, we have responsibility as well. Hillary Clinton famously wrote *It Takes a Village* to raise a child. Many of us hope that's true, because if it takes parents, then we're the ones ultimately responsible. Our happiness is no longer as important as our kids' is, and that's scary.

The second part of this ideology is that one's autonomy, and one's feelings, are sacred. If we spank, we infringe upon them. Instead, we should seek to validate kids' feelings. But feelings are not necessarily good. Kids may feel that they want to punch their sister, eat everybody's dessert, or be rude to Grandma and Grandpa. It doesn't matter how much I understand that my children want all the dessert; they're still not going to get it. And if I, as a parent, seek to understand them rather than to teach them that selfishness is bad, I've failed. Kids are not simply miniature adults; they are immature, often wrong, and they need our guidance. There are ways to offer it other than spanking, but the goal itself is good.

Many who oppose spanking wouldn't support these other trends, but this fight nevertheless is at the forefront of this movement. So I guess it all boils down to this: will outlawing spanking make the world safer for kids? Sweden has found the exact opposite, where rates of child abuse have increased sevenfold since its spanking ban. And if we create a society where parents begin to doubt their authority, we will endanger children. Kids need adult love and discipline to thrive.

But even more importantly, many children desperately do need society's protection. I hope that when the Supreme Court rules this week, they will make sure our resources are free to save these kids, rather than submitting children from loving homes to horrible ordeals just because their parents choose to spank.

*I ignored the letters to the editor after this one, but I was very happy to see the Supreme Court make a reasonable decision on this case. It seems*

*the Supremes, and most of society, agree with me.*
*So why can't we talk about it in polite society*
*without fearing being labelled a Neanderthal?*

## A Passion-Less Childhood
*This column was first published April 5, 2004*

*I*'m going to see *The Passion* for the second time this week. It will help me get in a more contemplative and grateful frame of mind for Easter, but I also want another opportunity to thank Mel. Mel Gibson looked at the movies offered to the public and saw that there was a huge segment of the population that was not being served by movies specializing in flatulence, car chases, and infidelity. So he made a meaningful movie instead.

In 1965, *The Sound of Music* won Best Picture. A majority of the American public actually went to see it. The audience for movies, though, has been steadily shrinking, with only about 20% of North Americans wandering into a theatre last year. That will change this year, since people who haven't seen a movie since Julie Andrews climbed every mountain are now flocking to see *The Passion*. My 95-year-old grandfather is even going. It's a powerful movie with an enduring message.

It's also incredibly violent. I figured I'd go, give Mel my money, and then spend the next two hours with my eyes closed. To my surprise, it wasn't that bad. It was brutal, but I have a much harder time watching movies where innocent bystanders are mowed down, or run over, or where children are kidnapped. I certainly closed my eyes at a few parts of *The Passion*, but overall I could manage it. The violence was historical, and it had purpose. It was similar to my reaction to *Schindler's List*, though far more intense since this suffering was specifically for me. I left the theatre wishing I could bring my daughters. If they were just a little older, I probably would. Perhaps that seems ghoulish, but it wasn't always so. After all, there were probably children watching the actual cross. Even two hundred years ago families would take their kids to see the latest hanging or, a hundred years before that, a good, gory drawing and quartering. Five hundred years ago entertainment was watching heretics being burned at the stake. The idea of shielding kids from violence is a fairly new phenomenon.

Perhaps that's because life today is so much easier. Not only were children of yesteryear exposed to violence, they were exposed to death. Most kids would have witnessed a death, since people tended to die at home, not in antiseptic nursing homes or hospitals. Many died when they were yet young of things that a simple prescription would take care of today. There was no escaping pain or violence or death.

I'm awfully glad my kids are shielded from that sort of thing, and perhaps even more glad that we've decided burning people at the stake was an overreaction. But the result is that we've created something called "childhood" that is unique to modern society. It's not just with regards to death, either. Young children were once expected to be useful. Three hundred years ago 10-year-old boys would be apprenticed away, living with a blacksmith, or a coppersmith, or a weaver. Even in the last century children worked alongside their parents on the farm as soon as they could be helpful, which was much younger than we would think. These kids were raised to work, unlike our own.

Today our children live lives where their main role is to play, with perhaps some school thrown in. It's a great life, and I'm glad we can give it to them. But at the same time, it means that life is not as serious. Kids may not be as prone to ask the big questions, to ensure they work hard, or to think about ethics as children may have been a century ago when much more was expected of them and when the reality of life and death stared them in the face.

I won't take my kids to see *The Passion* simply because they now live in a different culture, one in which such violence, no matter how meaningful, would be overwhelming. Maybe, though, we'll talk about it a little more this year. They will grow up soon enough. I just hope that they haven't been so sheltered that these difficult questions will always seem incomprehensible.

# How Virtue Triumphed
*This column was first published September 11, 2002*

As I watched the towers—and the world as we knew it—come crashing down last year, I called my kids to watch it with me. They did so in silence, sensing, I think, how monumental this act of war was. Perhaps it was the wrong decision, but I wanted to make sure they remembered September 11.

Yet the horror that was so stark on that first day was soon overshadowed by the stories of heroism. Firemen walked up the stairs to their deaths, passing others streaming down. Two stockbrokers carried their co-worker in her wheelchair down 90 flights of stairs. Todd Beamer recited the Lord's Prayer right before he rallied his co-passengers with "Let's Roll!" And 24-year-old equities trader Welles Crowther donned a red bandana and rushed from floor to floor guiding others, blinded by smoke, to exits. He, too, was last seen climbing the stairs.

> All character, whether good or bad, is formed by the choices we make in the little things.

It's those heroes we remember, much more so than the monsters that perpetrated the evil. I must admit I've spent precious little time over the last few years pondering Mohammed Atta and lots of time musing about Todd Beamer, Rudy Giuliani, or the men of Ladder 12. The reason they are so memorable, I think, is that they, rather than the terrorists, embody true humanity.

None of those individuals, though, set out to be heroes. They wanted to get home to their wives and kids as much as anyone else did. But they made their choices. They chose virtue, while the terrorists chose evil, just as terrorists have done since in Beslan, Madrid, Bali, and Moscow. September 11 was only the first to remind us all too vividly that evil is real. Yet though evil is most visible in barbaric acts as these, it rarely just erupts on the scene. On the contrary, it is cultivated in far smaller acts in our daily lives.

All character, whether good or bad, is formed by the choices we make in the little things. When we face a choice, if we choose right, virtue becomes a part of who we are. Good character, you see, is made, not born. Few kids develop good character by themselves; most need parents to point them towards that narrow road that, all too frequently now, is becoming less travelled by. This, too, is done in a series of small choices as we raise our kids. When we stop our kids from calling each other names, confront them when they're drowning in self-pity, or encourage them to share, we're cultivating virtue. Unfortunately, it takes a lot of work! It's easier to let things slide, to let the kids have petty fights, to listen to our teens gossip on the phone or to watch them exclude a neighbour without intervening. Yet when we do so, we're teaching them to disregard others and to focus on themselves. We are cultivating selfishness, not goodness.

Hard as it is to teach them right, it's even harder to model it! It means not griping about our boss, not cheating on our taxes, even loving and forgiving our spouse when we're ready to tear someone's head off.

If we have the stamina for this job, though, the payoff in future generations will be immense. For if our kids learn to choose right in the little things, then when the big things come they will also choose right. They will be faithful spouses. They will be loving, responsible parents. They will be honest neighbours. They will be caring citizens. They will be saving others from tears, heartache, or hardship as much as those on Flight 93 saved the targeted victims in Washington. For when we cultivate virtue in our kids, we aren't just teaching them to be kind; we are creating our future world.

I, for one, want to live in a world where people care for each other, where we come to a neighbour's aid, provide a shoulder to cry on, or respond to a call for help.

That world starts with me, with my kids, and with you and yours. Let's make the cultivation of virtue our legacy for 9/11. It triumphed on that day, and if we remain vigilant, it can triumph again.

*In the original column I did not name Welles Crowther. I talked about an equities trader donning a red bandana. This column was reprinted in a few American newspapers, and a while later I received an e-mail from Alison Crowther, Welles' mother. She told me she really appreciated the column and shared with me some of her thoughts and reactions on that day and the months that followed as her son's story became known. It was a humbling experience for me to talk to this woman who had lost so much and yet was still able to say she was glad her son had done what he did, despite the cost. You can find out more about Welles at www.redbandanna.org.*

# The Disappearance of Evil
*This column was first published September 29, 2003, in the middle of the provincial election*

When Steven Spielberg made *Schindler's List* in 1993, he did so because he didn't want people to forget the horrors of the Holocaust. At the time, I remember thinking that he was an incredibly paranoid man. Sure there are Holocaust deniers, but most people could never get over such atrocities.

Ten years later, I think he was incredibly prescient.

The change, though, is not with the increase in Holocaust deniers. It's with the increase in Holocaust "equivalizers," if I can make up a word. It's the tendency to label those viewpoints we don't like "evil" and those individuals we don't like "Nazis."

Elinor Caplan, then the Liberal Immigration Minister, said during the last election that those who voted for the Alliance were Holocaust deniers. Unions of all stripes called Mike Harris evil. In the current provincial election campaign, both sides are throwing the "evil" label at each other. And perhaps most famously, in the anti-war protests, signs spouted "Bush=Hitler."

I find this profoundly disturbing. It is as if, as a culture, we have lost our grip on evil. So let's refresh. (I'm sorry I'm going to be gruesome here, but I think it's necessary.) It was evil when Jewish parents had to surreptitiously hand their babies over to complete strangers to smuggle them out of Germany because it was the only hope their children had (they themselves had none). It was evil a few years later when they had to hold their other children as they gasped for the air that would not come. It is evil when a father in Iran beheads his 7-year-old daughter because he suspects she may have been raped. It is evil when warring factions kidnap 10- and 11-year-old girls to use them as sex slaves for their soldiers. It is evil when a mother drives her car into a lake with her sons strapped in the back seat because her new boyfriend doesn't want children. And it was evil when Saddam Hussein put his enemies in a shredder, feet first. It is evil when someone deliberately does harm for harm's sake.

Mike Harris never raped a little girl in front of her mother. He never killed anyone, tortured anyone, or chopped off any body parts. And Ernie Eves, his successor, has refrained from all these things, too. Bush has never tried to eradicate an entire race of people, and he has never left anyone to drown in a car (though a colleague in the Senate of a different political persuasion has).

Yet calling those we disagree with "evil" is easier than having to explain why their policies are wrong. The Conservatives wanted to cut welfare rates because they believed handing people money for nothing would perpetuate poverty, not end it. You can disagree with them all you want, but they were not evil. The Liberals, in advocating a different approach, similarly are not evil. One side is probably wrong, but let's debate the merits of the ideas, not call people names.

When we start calling everything evil, then nothing is evil. In the book *1984*, everything bad is "ungood," whether it's torture or a hangnail. And once everything is "ungood," then there is no word for the truly evil. It ceases to exist.

When I watched *Schindler's List*, the question that plagued me then, and still does now, is "what would I have done?" Would I have been part of the solution, or would I have turned away? I worry that our children won't even think to ask such a question, because we are erasing the whole concept of evil. The next time a Hitler or an Idi Amin or a Hussein come along, will our children even be able to recognize it? They'll hear these people called "evil," just as they heard George Bush, Dalton McGuinty, or Ernie Eves called evil. Deep inside, though, we all know these leaders aren't that bad. So these new tyrants probably aren't that bad, either. We have to put an end to this. For the world's sake, let's stop calling people names. Let's reserve "evil" for what is truly evil, and debate everyone else on their policies. It's called being civilized. Maybe we should give it a try.

*When the column appeared, it had the following disclaimer at the bottom:*

Sheila currently does not have a political sign on her lawn because she worries that the state of her lawn would cause people to vote the other way.

# Teens at the Ballot Box

*This column originally appeared June 7, 2004, in the middle of the federal election*

An election is coming, and for many teenagers it will be the first time they will vote in a federal election. For many more, it will be the first time they will skip voting in a federal election.

Young people, between the ages of 18–24, have the lowest voter turnout of any age group. In 2000, it was just under 40%, compared to 60% overall. Many lament this lack of civic spirit, but I'm not sure it's such a bad thing. In some ways, it's actually mature. They don't know much about politics or care much about politics, so why would they vote? It wouldn't be responsible. It's not so surprising, anyway. When you're that age, your most pressing concern is how to afford something to eat other than Spaghetti-O's while simultaneously trying to pay for your own apartment. You're so busy trying to figure out your life you don't have time to figure out a country. And don't worry; their time will come. When we were young, our generation didn't vote in that large numbers, either.

I actually wonder if perhaps this generation is the most honest generation when it comes to voting. At least they don't go through the motions if they don't really care. I think one reason political insults often get so extreme is because we don't necessarily want the details about the issues. We vote on impressions, not convictions. Politicians, then, spend a lot of time calling each other names instead of explaining why their policies are better. Besides, it creates much better sound bites than explaining how easing up on the monetary supply can affect the interest rate.

Nevertheless, if we could raise teens to care about the direction of their country—even if they don't see how it affects their menu choices beyond Spaghetti-O's—that obviously would be a good thing. After all, few have as much at stake in the election as the youth, who must live with whatever we do to this country for far longer than the rest of us.

How do we raise kids that care? I've been thinking about this lately, and when my girls are teenagers, even before they're allowed to vote, here's the election primer I'm going to use. First, take a week and read two different newspapers of different ideological bents. Then make a list of four or five issues that really matter to you: taxes, the deficit, the economy, the military, social concerns like gay marriage, health-care management, Quebec—anything that you think is vital. Make a chart with the three parties and write down what each would propose to do about these things. You can often get this information from their Web sites, and that's something any teenager can manage!

Now comes the tough part. Which solution sounds the most feasible? One that involves more money? Less money? What about real structural change? Don't take the politicians' word for it; think about it.

Once the issues are out of the way, we come to the "would you want to invite this person over for a barbecue" test. As soon as a politician calls someone names rather than dealing with the issues, I immediately answer "no." Then there's the "icky" factor. Do you trust this person? Bill Clinton admits that his affair with Lewinsky distracted him from his job—even when it was just the two of them and before it became front-page news. I don't want a leader who's going to be distracted by something or someone—or trying to cover something up.

None of this research needs to take very much time. Any teenager can do it by reading the papers for a week and surfing the Net for half an hour. If your teen doesn't want to do it alone, you can always do it together. Of course, the things that matter to you may not matter to him or her. Yet what a great wake-up call for teens! They'll see that if they don't vote when it's their turn, people like their parents will run the country. We may not think that's such a bad idea, but if it motivates young people to adopt true civic responsibility, bring it on.

# Burqhas and Bra Straps
*This column originally appeared February 24, 2003*

Last month, eighteen women in Afghanistan were allowed to take their driver's tests. When reading the news account, what struck me was not their amazing liberation, though, but the reason they wanted to drive in the first place: to stop the unrelenting sexual harassment as they walked down the street—get ready for it—in their *burqhas*. Now I can't think of anything sexier than that, can you? For all you know, she might have three eyes, a warty nose, and seventeen fingers under all that, but hubba hubba!

In those societies, a woman is so dangerous that she has to be covered so as not to incite men's uncontrollable urges. Well, obviously it's not working. Women evidently need more covering. Perhaps they could attach rods to their heads, from which they could hang curtains. They would be a six-foot-square walking box, maybe with a periscope on top so they can see out. Would that halt the temptation?

> **We are asking an awful lot of teenage boys, while asking hardly anything of girls.**

But as ridiculous as I think it is to blame women for men lusting after them, sometimes I wonder if we haven't gone too far in the other direction. I remember as a teenager dressing without giving any thought to what effect it would have on hormone-raging 17-year-old boys whose thoughts, approximately every 2.3 seconds, apparently turn to sex. My eyes were opened when I was married and Keith would comment favourably on some outfit I had once worn. I'd look at him in amazement and say, "But, darling, that made my knees look fat." He'd look at me equally bewildered and reply, "Honey, fat was the farthest word from my mind."

I have never been a teenage boy. I have never even played one on TV. But I'm married to someone who once was one, and in conversations with him and with other couples, all the men have said, without exception, "It is so hard to learn math when someone is sitting next to you with a low-cut top and a miniskirt." And all of us women looked at these neanderthals incredulously for thinking that way.

But apparently boys do think that way, no matter how pathetic we women think that is. And girls imperil themselves when they forget that. I know older generations have been complaining about what teenagers wear forever (Honey, that mammoth skin draws too much attention to your cleavage), but perhaps we need to give this some consideration. We are asking an awful lot of teenage boys, while asking hardly anything of girls. When I was in high school, the height of social embarrassment was if your bra strap was showing. Today, that's stylish, as if we really need to remind boys what's underneath our tops. Personally, I don't think most girls intend to be sexually provocative. I think they honestly just want to be "pretty." But if pretty now means jeans cut low enough around your hips that you can see the top of thong underwear, then maybe we need to change our definition.

It's not only clothes, though. In California, a 17-year-old was recently convicted of rape in the following case: A girl invited him and his friend into a private bedroom, where they proceeded to do some pretty grown-up things together. One boy completed the act and left. The other boy then commenced, but several minutes later the girl said, "Um, I think I should be going now." The judges decided this boy was supposed to interpret her comment as "stop now" and calmly cease and desist. He certainly should have. But he's a 17-year-old in the middle of a rather exciting act. We're putting girls in a lot of danger when we tell them that boys will always stop even if the engine's going, that it's never the girls' responsibility to stall that engine in the first place. We're teaching our daughters to trust boys to stop, even if our daughters dress unwisely, talk unwisely, and act unwisely.

Maybe it's time dads—or other important males—sat down with girls and told them exactly what teenage boys are thinking. Burqhas are evil, but Britney Spears' fashion sense probably doesn't contribute much to the public good, either. Let's find a balance we can all live with, and then maybe math scores would finally start rising again.

*The reactions to this column were interesting. Many moms of teenage boys contacted me to thank me. A lot of women, though, were offended. They said women had fought long and hard for the right to wear whatever they wanted without being told they were asking to be raped. I certainly understand that. But we also need to use a little common sense, and a little decency. I don't think women really understand the way male brains work. In an ideal world, women could wear whatever they wanted, walk when it's dark outside by themselves, get drunk without having to worry that someone may take advantage of them, or go into a man's apartment on their own without fear of attack. But this isn't an ideal world, and I think it's much better to teach our girls to function and protect themselves in this world, even if we wish it could be different.*

# Lingerie Lite

*A version of This column was first published December 8, 2003. In that one I did not name names of shops. The editors felt that may be ill-advised, shall we say. But I'm going to do so here. This is the one I wanted to see printed.*

$\mathcal{I}$ have a very dear five-year-old friend named Paul. He's so cute that whenever you see him, you have to squeeze him. At school, he can't go down the hall without girls pinching his cheeks or hugging him. One day last year his mother Lisa found him sniffling after school, and after some gentle prodding, the problem was revealed: "Mommy, I just can't decide who I'm going to marry." It seems the poor soul had had several girls tell him they wanted to marry him, and he didn't want to disappoint anyone.

In all likelihood, Paul won't be getting married for at least two decades. But nevertheless, our schoolchildren seem to spend an inordinate amount of time talking about their "boyfriends" or "girlfriends" or who they have a crush on—when they're 5! They don't even know what to do with a crush, but they know they should have one. Instead of just enjoying being kids, they're playing being grown-up.

Parents may laugh at our little ones, saying things like, "Isn't that cute? She has a little boyfriend." And perhaps I'm overreacting and most of this is harmless enough. But let me just have my moment of motherly regret that we can't keep our kids kids any more. They're so busy trying to act like grown-ups that they don't just play. It's hard enough not having a boyfriend or girlfriend when you're 17. Do 7-year-olds have to start worrying about it, too?

Part of the problem, I think, is the steady sexualization of girls, growing ever younger every year. First graders come to school donning spaghetti straps and exposed navels. Eight-year-olds wear jeans riding down like Britney Spears. Looking grown-up now means looking sexy, even before many of these little girls know what that word means.

Every time I go to the mall, I have to shake my head in disbelief at La Senza Girl. Before the protests start, perhaps they do have some lovely clothes, but let's get one thing straight: it's named after a lingerie store! There's nothing wrong with a store selling sexy lingerie, of course. But why should we have a store aimed at 6–12-year-olds named after it?

Its parent store isn't much better. Outside La Senza right now is a large poster of a young woman dressed in high heels, lacy underwear that barely covers anything, and nothing else. It simply isn't the kind of picture you would want your daughters to see (let alone your 13-year-old boys). They could always move it inside the store, but head office wants it outside, where everyone on their way to the food court will see it. You can't even avoid these images by walking on the other side of the hallway, either. Opposite La Senza is Ardene, a store catering to young teens, which promotes itself via a picture of a topless girl with her jeans unbuttoned and unzipped. What message is that supposed to send?

Though things are getting worse, it's not an entirely new phenomenon. Barbie is over 50 years old, and she's best known for her outrageous proportions. Did you know that if Barbie were life-sized, her measurements would be 44-12-22? She wouldn't even be able to stand up! My own daughters' measurements are 21-21-21. For a while we had our daughters addicted to Groovy Girls, whose most bizarre physical trait is the size of their feet. But alas, my girls have abandoned these cute little dolls in favour of the mutant Barbie once again.

It's hard to avoid it. All around us advertising, stores, and even toys remind girls that being "sexy" matters. Yet I want my daughters to stay little girls as long as they can. And that means staying away from lingerie lite. So this year, I'm going to do something about it. I'm going to call La Senza and tell them to move that poster inside the store. I'll say, "If you want to sell sex to my kids, you're not going to sell anything to me." Why don't you join me so we can really make a difference? Their number is 1-888-527-3692. Our kids deserve better.

## A Prom Tale
*This column was first published July 26, 2004*

*L*et me tell you a story...
Michelle and Kaitlyn stood in front of the mirror, thrilled with their prom dresses. This was their big night.

"We have a deal, right?" Kaitlyn asked. Michelle nodded. If the drinking got out of hand, they would call a cab together. It wasn't that Michelle disagreed with drinking. It's just that the one time she did, she got sick and blacked out. It scared her, and she didn't want to wreck her big night.

Craig and Jeff soon arrived to pick them up. She and Craig had been dating since September. He was wonderful, though she wasn't sure about their future. Michelle had been accepted into nursing at Queen's. Craig wasn't going to school. She worried they might grow apart, but her negative thoughts evaporated when she saw the hall where Centennial was having its 2004 prom. Over at her table her friends were already laughing, holding up shot glasses. Michelle was surprised; why did they have shot glasses inside? But apparently the shot glasses were party favours, given to everyone by the prom committee.

Then she saw the rest of the package. There was a MADD key chain, a quarter, and a condom. Michelle's cheeks went red. Whatever happened to a coffee mug filled with chocolates, or a commemorative picture frame? She'd been pushing Craig away for weeks whenever he tried to go too far, but now she saw him flicking the condom in the air. Other couples around the hall were already making out. Michelle's skin went cold. Everyone expected her to say yes tonight.

> **Then she saw the rest of the package. There was a MADD key chain, a quarter, and a condom.**

They danced, and she soon managed to relax and enjoy the evening. Craig was treating her royally. He held the chair out. He told her again and again that he loved her. She had never felt so special.

As he ushered her out a few hours later, she passed Kaitlyn. By the way Jeff was swaying, it was obvious he'd been filling that shot glass. "Are you guys coming with us to Sharon's?" Jim asked. Kaitlyn's eyes pleaded with Michelle, saying, "we had a deal, remember?" But

Craig was already pushing Michelle towards his car. "I guess not," Michelle shouted over her shoulder.

It's only another party, she told herself. But that wasn't all it was. Craig had arranged for a room alone. And at that late hour, with the music still in the air, she couldn't find a reason to say no. Everybody was doing it, after all. She wasn't a prude.

Afterwards she felt hollow. It had been uncomfortable and Craig hadn't cared. He hadn't even stayed with her. He was already in another room drinking. Michelle rushed downstairs, makeup streaming, to call a cab.

The significance of the sirens she heard didn't register until they passed the accident site. There was Jeff's car, wrapped around a tree.

All of that was three years ago. Michelle turned the key in the ignition as she pulled out of Kaitlyn's parents' driveway, following her monthly visit to her paralyzed friend. They had had a deal.

She looked at herself in the rearview mirror. Would this ever end? For Kaitlyn it wouldn't. She herself had felt sick ever since her gynecological rotation last month. All the stats ran through her brain continuously, like a bad song. Condoms don't protect against HPV, which can cause cancer. Chlamydia...infertility...ectopic pregnancies. She knew the chances were still in her favour, but she still wished she could go back to those two giddy friends, looking at their dresses in the mirror.

The people in this story are fictional. The party favours given out at the Centennial prom this year are not. Certainly many teens will engage in these behaviours on prom night. That does not mean, however, that they should be encouraged, especially when such things may be dangerous, and in many cases illegal. High schools have washed their hands of the prom, allowing students to run it themselves. By so doing, they abdicate their responsibility, ensuring that no adults actually supervise it. They throw kids like Michelle and Kaitlyn, who want to say no, into a very difficult situation. If your child is entering his or her senior year, perhaps you should ask who is supervising the prom and what, exactly, will be on those prom tables.

*I don't think any column has ever received the reaction this one did. People wrote in on all sides to the paper, some calling me old-fashioned and some lauding me for being courageous. Those on the prom committee, obviously, weren't very happy with me. Many teens wrote to say that I had wrecked their prom. It had been a wonderful night, and now everyone was talking about it as if it had been horrible. However, I only wrote this column because teens came to me to complain and asked me to get the word out. I'm sure many teens did have a wonderful time at the prom, and I'm glad they did. But not everyone did. If changing the party favours could help those who were offended and uncomfortable have a better time next year, then that may be a good step to ensuring everyone has a wonderfully memorable night.*

# A Kick in the Head?

*This column was first published August 16, 2004*

 y recent column regarding the ill-advised party favours at a local prom (a condom and a shot glass, among others) has inspired a number of letters, both good and bad. Another columnist claimed I obviously felt that today's teens were going to "heck" in a handbasket, as if what they really needed was a good kick in the head. However, I'd be inclined to point my boot elsewhere.

The problem with today's teens is not that they're making bad decisions; actually, their decisions, on the whole, are much better than we would expect. It's instead that they've been dealt a much harder deck than other generation in recent history.

If today's teens are sexually active, they are far more likely to contract an STD, largely because our generation has been so sexually promiscuous that such diseases are now common. Indeed, sexual behaviour is on parade everywhere in the media, telling us promiscuity is normal and even good, largely because we—the adults—watch this stuff! If we didn't go to graphic movies or cruise the Internet for pornography, the supply would dry up. If we stopped watching inane sitcoms, advertisers would pull their ads and networks would have to come up with something else. If we parents refused to shop at stores that sexualized preteen girls, stores would stop doing it.

It's not just that we've permitted society to go downhill, though. We've allowed our families to go downhill, too. Today's teens are products of parents who, in large numbers, have chosen work over parenthood. We've decided, as a generation, that our children need bigger houses, better entertainment equipment, and nicer vacations, rather than more time to play Monopoly together. One study showed that the average parent spends just 38 minutes per week talking to their children!

Then, instead of working on our marriages, we've allowed them to disintegrate, leaving kids without the security of an intact family. (I'm talking in societal terms rather than individual terms; many single parents, obviously, did not choose to be that way.) Those who don't have primary custody of their children have, in large numbers, abandoned those children, leaving a hole in their children's lives no one else can fill.

In all these things, whether it's media or work or family, many of us are just as trapped as our teens are. We have gone along with society and yet have not found the promised happiness. For all our work, and consumerism, and pursuing our own dreams, we largely haven't found peace because we've forgotten the real source for happiness.

So today, when our teens enter high school, they often have little parental guidance. At the same time, they're surrounded by media that glorifies the same dysfunction that has failed us. Is it any wonder that teens make bad decisions? What is a wonder, to me, is that so many teens make good ones. It's as if they looked at their parent's generation and found it wanting, and have decided that their lives are not going to look like that. Juvenile crime is down. Drug use and alcohol abuse is down. And authority is up! Around 70% of teens actually crave more advice from their parents about sex and other difficult issues, not less. Are we listening?

In fact, they crave family, period. Over 42% of them say they want three or more children, and want them within marriage. They have a more conservative view about sex, too. In a recent poll, adults were asked whether or not it would be embarrassing for a teen to admit he or she was a virgin. Half of adults believed it would be, but it seems only a quarter of their children share that view. They're demonstrating this in their behaviour. Ten years ago, 54% of teenagers were sexually active; 46% were not. Today those numbers are reversed.

These kids have watched their parents' lives be devastated by divorce, workaholism, and misplaced priorities. Many want no part of it. What I hope and pray is that we as parents, aunts and uncles, neighbours, grandparents and friends can stand alongside them and support them, rather than undermining them as we did at that prom.

No, we don't owe today's teens a kick in the head. We owe them an apology.

# *A* Mother's Heart

I'm a writer, a speaker, a wife, a daughter, a friend. But ask me how I most think of myself and I will say, "I'm a mom." I love being a mom. It's not always easy, but motherhood fills your heart with such love, that little else in the world could. The columns in this chapter can be divided into two categories: those that deal with sorting out our roles as moms and those that deal with the heartaches a mom can face. I hope other moms—and even dads—enjoy them.

## Banishing the Stay-at-Home Blues

*This column was first published April 14, 2003*

*I*f you judge by the comments of many of my acquaintances, I have the personality of a pea. If you're a stay-at-home parent, you know what I mean. People constantly remark, "I don't know how you do it. I would go stir-crazy if I had to stay home with my kids." The inference, of course, is that I am some sort of mutant subspecies that requires far less intellectual stimulation than normal and can survive for days on end with the praise from Barney—"I love you; you love me."

It's time to challenge this notion that staying home with your kids is akin to a prison sentence with an awfully whiny jailer. Certainly it can be tremendously difficult, draining, and exhausting, especially since you usually walk around with banana mash on your jeans and spit up on your sweatshirt. But that's not the whole story.

Many parents choose to work for a host of different reasons, and only you know what is right for your family. I know that for many, much as you may long to, staying home isn't financially feasible. But if it's possible in your situation to be home even part-time, I'd like to put in a plug in for it, and to tell you that it doesn't need to be as difficult as it sounds.

**Staying at home with your kids is wonderful, but it will not meet all your needs.**

First, I think we go about stay-at-home parenting all wrong. We start by buying tons of equipment (ExerSaucers, swing sets, trampolines) to ensure that we never have to leave the house. But what happens if we're home alone all the time? Our kids may go stir-crazy and whine, cry, and vomit. Then we cry. Probably we whine, too. And if we're pregnant, we definitely vomit.

So let's take a step back and approach this stay-at-home thing differently. We commonly think it has to meet all our needs, because parenting is *so* great. We cocoon ourselves in our homes, thinking bliss will greet us, and when it doesn't and we're ready to drop that hair dryer into that bathtub, we wonder what's wrong with us.

Staying at home with your kids is wonderful, but it will not meet all your needs. You don't need to feel guilty about it. Yet if you acknowledge what your needs are, and plan for them, you *can* meet your needs while you stay at home.

The first thing we need is adult conversation (that Barney thing only works for so long). Take your kids to a playgroup, or organize one yourself. Join the local YMCA or another fitness club that offers babysitting. Check into Early Learning Centres in your area. Just make sure you do something every day!

How about intellectual stimulation? You definitely don't need a job for this! Start a new hobby, like gardening or quilting. Take your kids to the library, and visit the adult department while you're there. Learn to trace your family tree, invest, or save money. Even if you only have time to read while sitting in the bathtub after the kids are in bed, you're giving yourself something new to think about. (Just don't drop the book. I've paid the library big bucks for this transgression.)

Finally, what about a sense of accomplishment? At work we get praise for finishing something. At home we get whines and piles of laundry that never get folded. If you want to feel like you've accomplished something, volunteer. Meet your neighbours and see if you can lend a hand to some older people or other struggling parents. Invite people over for coffee. They won't mind the mess nearly as much as you think they will! And the more connection you have with your community, the more you'll realize the difference you can make in people's lives.

I do not have the personality of a pea. I'd say it's more like a bunch of grapes (the seedless kind), with many different things in my life that are all interconnected. It is such a privilege to stay at home and watch my children grow. They are my reward. But I could not survive without acknowledging that though I love being a mommy best, I am more than that. Plan for success when you stay at home. Don't settle for exhaustion. Your life will be richer for it.

*My father-in-law read this column and said, "Will you stop talking about vomit!" He can say that. It's been twenty years since he had little kids at home and even longer since his wife was pregnant. Ask me again in ten years, and maybe I'll have a different answer.*

## Paying to Stay at Home
*This column was first published January 20, 2003*

I'm a wee mite upset. The federal government recently announced that it has earmarked half a billion dollars to expand daycare, along with another $1 billion to expand the child tax benefit, labelling them both *new children's initiatives*. Now, I can see the justification for the latter, and any other initiative that gives parents a bit of a break. We are, after all, raising the generation that will staff our nursing homes and hospitals when we need them. But is increasing daycare actually aimed at helping kids?

It seems to me that the government has decided to help a certain type of family—namely one who uses daycare centres—instead of helping all Canada's children. Now I know many single-parent families require daycare, but the majority of users of daycare centres are not single parents but parents from dual earning households. So couples where both parents work are going to benefit most from this initiative. The government, though, already subsidizes this type of family big time.

Consider a two-earner family with $10,000 in child care expenses where one spouse makes $40,000 and the other $30,000. That family pays $11,652 in taxes (stats courtesy of the Fraser Institute). Their neighbours, where one parent works earning $60,000 and one parent stays at home, have the same pre-tax income (since they don't pay for child care), but they're paying $16,037 in taxes. They're paying over $4,000 more, so in effect they're helping to pay for their neighbour's child-care while they're not even getting any breaks on their own costs.

Sure this is unfair, but if the government were the only entity that could produce quality daycare centres, then this new expansion may still be justified. But this is the government that gave us the human resources job scandal and the gun registry scandal. That's over $2 billion down the toilet already. Do you really trust them with your money, let alone your children?

Besides, let's look at how well the government handles schools. According to the Cato Institute, the average private school tuition in North America is just over $4,000.00 Canadian. The average public school cost per capita in Ontario, though, is $7,000. Yet private school students do better by every measure, primarily because the money goes to the classroom instead of to administration (can anyone say *gun registry*?).

And it's not just because families who use private schools are better. In American communities where vouchers have been instituted, children from the lowest classes have done far better when permitted to attend a private school than when they stayed in public schools. (I don't have room to go into this in detail, but maybe I will in another column!)

Government ineptitude, though, isn't the only problem. By focusing on daycare centres, the government has decided not only to fund one particular type of family but also one particular type of child care arrangement. My brother- and sister-in-law have worked opposite shifts for years so someone's always home with the kids. Where's their money? Or what if you want to hire your sister to babysit because she loves your kids almost as much as you do? Zilch for you, too.

By funding only daycare centres, the government essentially is telling us how to best manage our families. Well, here's a radical idea: how about letting us decide? If the government really wants to help kids, why not give that money back to all parents through refundable tax credits.

A lot of us would spend the money on daycare centres, and more would open to meet this increased demand. But some of us might also spend money moving to a nicer neighbourhood. Some of us may simply use it on groceries and heat. And some of us may use it so that one parent can stay at home.

And therein lies the problem. The current government believes it knows what will benefit families far better than the families themselves do. But we all have different circumstances and different needs. If the government wants to support families monetarily, that's fine. But surely we should at least have the choice how it should be done. They are, after all, our children.

# A Mother's Day Pep Talk

*This column was first published May 12, 2003*

On Sunday many of you were greeted in bed with awful coffee, cold toast, and soggy cereal. Having been forced many times to eat the "Breakfast of Champions" after it has congealed into a solid mass, I find it hard to decide if we "breakfast in bed" moms are the lucky ones or if the ones who prepared their own coffee are more fortunate. But nevertheless, Sunday was our day.

And I think we needed it. In fact, I think we need a lot more pampering, because being a mom is awfully hard. Part of the reason is that you're not just a mother. You're also a psychologist, a manager, a nurse, a maid, a chauffeur, a teacher, an activities coordinator, a referee, a cook, and, somewhere in your spare time, perhaps even a wife.

So if you feel like you're going full speed ahead and you're sure you would have crashed long ago if only you'd had the time, you're not alone. That's the normal mode for us today. The reason you feel out of control is not that something's wrong with you; it's that something's wrong with our whole society. How many things on this list drive you nuts? Driving your children back and forth between karate classes, swimming lessons, and Boy Scouts? Cleaning up hundreds of pieces of Lego and playdough off of the floor? Trying to get your kids unglued from the TV or the Nintendo so they can shovel some food into their faces before they return to the tube?

Well, believe it or not, mothers even thirty years ago didn't have to deal with any of these things. Kids a generation ago had after-school activities, but they were called "go and play with your friends down the street until supper" instead of "Boy Scouts" or "gymnastics lessons." Kids had fewer toys. They didn't have Nintendo. And in most houses, it was still assumed that kids would do some chores. Today, we're happy if they clear a path to their room once in a while.

It doesn't stop there. Everything also conspires to make us feel like outsiders in our kids' lives. Many of us work shift work, so we can't be home with our kids as much as we would like. Friends steal kids away. TV steals them away. The Internet lets them "chat" with whomever they want—except you. And on TV, mothers are often portrayed as clueless or as obstacles to kids' happiness. Even schools can make us feel belittled by doing much of our job for us. They don't just teach kids to read—at least, we hope they teach kids to read—they also teach them about sex, drugs, and alcohol. They help them with career planning. They prepare them for the future. We're left supporting the schools, rather than the schools supporting us.

On Mother's Day, then, if you're wondering if you're up to the task, take a deep breath and RELAX. It's only natural to feel exhausted and out of touch. There is nothing wrong with you. But at the same time let's not accept defeat! Don't let all these pressures stop you from doing what you know is right for your kids. It's so easy when we feel distant to want to close that gap and be buddy-buddy with our children. But your kids don't need you as a friend; they have lots of friends. They need you as a mom, because you're the only one they've got.

They want you more than they want karate classes, more than gourmet dinners, and more than the latest

Nintendo. You are the best one to help your children succeed, motivate them to try, and help form their morals, because you are their mother. No one, no matter how well meaning, loves your children more than you do. So don't be intimidated. Love them, but set limits, too. Say no to more activities. Switch off the TV and have dinner together. Play with them. It's the most important job you have, the one with the most rewards, and the one that only you can do. Children may not say it, but they need you. And they love you. And deep inside, they're glad you're there.

## Mothering on a Weak Stomach
*This column was first published May 10, 2004*

*I* have often marvelled at the fact that my youngest daughter is so healthy. At first I chalked it up to home-schooling, since we shelter her from germ factories. But thanks to Austrian lung specialist Dr. Friedrich Bischinger, I now have the real answer. It turns out that picking your nose and eating it boosts the immunity.

This is one of those things that, as a parent, you would rather not know. And as I was pondering this piece of research, a few questions occurred to me. Does Bischinger have nothing better to do with his time than worry about nose picking? Perhaps he should come do a shift or two at Canadian hospitals and fill in for some of the overworked internists here.

Even more importantly, how does one measure this particular experiment? You have to compare the pick-and-swallow kids with something. Do you arrange for a group of pick-and-stick-it-on-the-side-of-Grandma's-couch? Or a group of non-pickers? In our family the question may be moot anyway, because we have actually cured my youngest of this habit, at least in public. According to Bischinger, of course, we should just let her rip. Somehow I just don't think I can find the stomach for it.

Stomach fortitude, though, is something I have discovered in a whole new way since becoming a mom. Grown women venture out with other grown women, only to find the conversation turning to the consistency of toddlers' fecal matter. Two or three years earlier many of us wouldn't even admit we had fecal matter. Kids, of course, don't share our squeamishness. They know body functions are taboo, but these still cause gales of laughter. They are the source of the most outrageous insults and humour they can imagine. (Typical joke told by a four-year-old: "Knock knock." "Who's there?" "Fart!"—followed by everyone collapsing on the floor laughing.)

> **Stomach fortitude, though, is something I have discovered in a whole new way since becoming a mom.**

Recently, when our family was considering renting a particular movie, I refused since it had swearing in it. Rebecca, our oldest, leaned over to her younger sister and whispered, "That means it has bum words."

The odd thing is that children have no concept of what actually is distasteful. They think nothing of barging into the bathroom at that particular moment when you really want privacy, but should they see you and your spouse kissing, well, the screams you hear are enough to think we had been the ones nose-picking.

Mealtimes are perhaps the worst for these expressions of disgust. I actually enjoy cooking, but my meals usually have vegetables and meat—I know this will be hard to believe—mixed together. This is a major faux pas in my children's eyes, and worthy of several choruses of "eeeewwww!" If everything is not confined to its own hemisphere on the plate, it's not worthy. And don't even get me started on sauces.

Yet I am not the only source of squeamish stomachs in our family. My daughters cause plenty of nausea, too. One of them, who has never met a sauce she likes, thinks nothing of picking up the gum she stuck on her dresser before dinner to finish it afterwards (we're working on curing her of that, too). And why is it so hard to get kids to remember to flush the toilet?

It seems that motherhood is an inauguration into new challenges for the stomach-challenged, which is probably why it begins as it does. When I was pregnant with Rebecca the only thing I thought of, for the first five months, was food. I dreamed about food. I daydreamed about food. The only thing I didn't do was eat food. I was so nauseated that every waking minute was dedicated to trying to picture some food that would stay down—an apple? A hard-boiled egg? Definitely nothing with sauce.

One day I will have the bathroom to myself, I will be able to kiss my husband whenever I want, eat whatever I want, and ignore the consistency of everybody's toilet habits. I think I'll miss these days. And that's why I still cherish the mushy kisses and mushy cereal I'm presented with every Mother's Day morning. I hope you all had a wonderful day Sunday, too.

## Too Busy Syndrome
*This column was first published September 15, 2003*

Last week, while filing away all my columns from this summer, I made a startling realization. Boy, am I grumpy. It's not that I disagree with any of them (I don't), it just seems like I spent my summer upset about things. Yet when I think back, I don't remember being particularly angry. On the whole, I had a wonderful summer visiting friends and camping. It was rustic; we were hardly ever home; and I was out in the wilderness with my girls, my husband, and no phone or computer. It was heaven.

But achieving that heavenly bliss required an awful lot of work. When I *was* home, I had to do mountains of everyone's laundry, pack up all the coolers again, sort all the mail, and, of course, write three or four columns over two days. I was busy. Very busy. And when I get busy, I get grumpy. I don't notice the good things around me. I only notice the things that annoy me.

My kids have realized this long ago. They know how to tell the days when I am suffering from TBS (Too Busy Syndrome), which makes PMS pale in comparison. When I am busy, my kids get yelled at a lot more. If they happen to do something outrageously kidlike, such as, for instance, play, and then they dare to enter another room without picking up their toys, they hear about it. "Are you trying to make more work for me? Do you know how much I have to get done today? I can't live like this!" And my girls peek at each other over their bowed heads and drag themselves over to clean up. Do I feel vindicated? No, I feel guilty. But it doesn't stop the grouch from peering her ugly head again when my husband gets home.

And complaining's not all I do. When I'm grouchy, I also order everyone else around. Some days, I think "Hurry up, we've got to go, hurry up!" are the only words out of my mouth. So this year, I have decided to take TBS by the horns. I don't want to be too busy. I'm sure my kids don't want me to be grumpy. So we're going to relax, darn it, even if it kills us.

That, of course, is not as easy as it sounds. If we're going to be Good Parents, you see, common wisdom has it that our children must be in 17 different after-school activities. They need extra stimulation. Sitting around the house is a sure sign of laziness. It's time we get serious about this kid business!

But what if the best thing we could do for our kids is to give them that time just to sit around the house? To do nothing in particular, and in the process maybe we'll play a game or chat while we're making cookies (I don't make cookies during my TBS days). These are the ways kids learn to feel safe, valued, and loved, and it builds their foundation for the future. All the karate classes, gymnastics lessons, and piano lessons in the world can't equal snuggling time with Mom and Dad. So we're going to choose one or two things the kids really love, and let the rest go.

Now that school has begun, our instinct, though, is to do the exact opposite. It's easy to think that this year we're going to get our act together and accomplish so much more. But the homework load will only get heavier as the months go on. Let's not set ourselves up for disaster now by taking on more than we can handle.

Last year, at our house, we did too many lessons. And when the kids weren't at lessons, Keith and I were at committee meetings. This year, many of these committees are going to have to survive without us. We have more important things to do. Like absolutely nothing. And maybe, when I conquer TBS, I'll be able to notice all the good things around me once again.

*I have not yet completely conquered TBS. Just when I think I have it licked, other things sneak into my schedule to replace the ones I've gotten rid of. But I'm working on it.*

## Who's to Blame?

*This column was first published May 3, 2004*

When Rebecca first learned to walk, I gloated. The other kids at our playgroup were still crawlers. My baby was obviously superior and, by extension, so was I.

A year later the situation reversed itself. All of the other kids were correctly vocalizing, "Mommy, want juice! Want juice!" while my child was pointing at a dog and grunting "woof woof" without the vowel sounds. Animal noises she had mastered, but words she would not say. For several months this rendered me mildly neurotic, as I wondered where I had gone wrong.

It's easy to take pride in our children's accomplishments, feeling that they somehow reflect well on our ability to parent. How do we handle it, though, when our children show weaknesses? It's one thing, too, if a child has trouble learning to speak correctly; we may excuse that (though a mother-in-law might not). Yet what about when behaviour problems enter the picture? What do we do when missing vowel sounds are no longer our biggest worry?

There's no doubt that parenting plays a huge role in how our children turn out. Last week I wrote about how we can influence the paths our children choose. Yet even if we do everything right, there are no guarantees. We certainly can increase the likelihood they'll do well, but there's still that pesky variable called choice that, much as we may like to, we can't swat like a bug.

Perhaps, as parents, we are both too quick to accept accolades when our children do well and too quick to accept blame when they do not. Part of this, I think, is an attempt to swat that bug. After all, if we're to blame for our children's mistakes, then it naturally follows that if we try hard enough we can fix the problem. We're the cause of it, so we must have the solution, if we can only stumble upon the right one. We want the world this way because it means we have control over our kids. But it's just an illusion. These little tiny babies that we brought into the world, naked and squirming, eventually grow up to make their own choices. We can't be totally to blame, or totally to praise, for the final product.

One of my high school friends came from a perfect family of five kids. They ate dinner together every night. They played board games and football together.

They read novels together. It was idyllic. But the third son apparently didn't see the family in these rosy hues and so he left home early, landing himself in various degrees of trouble. The other four, on the other hand, were model citizens. Same family, different outcomes. The only variable, as far as I could see, was choice.

Unfortunately, friends and family members—especially family members—act as if there *are* guarantees. If your child talks back to you in public, isn't toilet trained by 3, doesn't get straight A's, or lives in her room with the door closed, it must be your fault. They may not say that, exactly, but they'll offer helpful tips that show their bias. "You know, when my kids were little, we didn't have these problems. I just wouldn't stand for it." You might have felt like replying, "Yes, but your kids didn't have spines," but you don't, because deep inside you wonder if they're right.

We all make mistakes when we parent, and happily most of these can be forgiven. Some, though, do have lasting consequences, throwing us into spirals of both worry and guilt. If you're engulfed in that right now, remember that you are not omnipotent. For good or evil, children are not mini-me's. Ultimately their choices reflect most specifically upon themselves. Let's do all we can to steer them well, for we do have much influence. But if your children are aging, your power is dwindling, and the future looks bleak, remember that you cannot change the past. What you can do is love and support your children in the most appropriate way today, hoping and praying that they will one day steer themselves on the right road.

*This column meant a lot to a family member. My mother-in-law cuts out all my columns and sends*

*them "down home" to New Brunswick, where
there are a few towns completely populated by
people who are related to my children in some
way. I'm glad this relative found this helpful,
and I hope others did, too.*

## A Grandmother's Tears
*This column was first published January 12, 2004*

What should a parent do if a child is having a tantrum, kicking and screaming for something you know is not in that child's best interests? The answer seems quite straightforward if one assumes this child is two. But what if the child is 24, and is having conniptions because you've tentatively suggested that perhaps he might consider paying a bit of rent, since you give him a roof, do his laundry, make his meals, and take his messages while he "works on his music." Actually, the answer is probably the same: take away his toys and deny privileges (in this case, the roof).

But let's throw a wrench in the works. What if the narcissistic child also has children of her own? What if denying privileges won't just impact her but also the babies she carelessly brought into the world? It's a dilemma faced by many grandparents today. These grandmas and grandpas thought their childrearing years were over, but now they want nothing more than custody of their grandchildren to protect these babies from their parents.

I have recently heard the stories of two such grandmothers, who, with their husbands, are caring for grandchildren whenever it suits the mothers' whims. Let me paint a picture of these mothers, for they are remarkably similar (I'll even pretend they're one). When she hit high school, she started abusing some substance or other and started hanging out with some guy with tattoos and rings and chains whose longest sentence on record was "Hey." Feeling this gentleman possessed superior genetic material, she wound up pregnant and moved out. But she didn't stay out. Once the baby was a few months old, she handed the child over to Grandma so she "could get her life together."

Then, a few months later, she took the baby back, applied for welfare, and continued to date a steady stream of undesirables (this time they had graduated to "What's up?"). In one case she got pregnant again. In the other case she got pregnant three more times. And every few nights she would call, demanding babysitting so she could go to a party. If the grandmother refused, the daughter took the children with her.

Soon the requests for money came. The grandmothers realized that if they didn't pay, these daughters would move in with Mr. Talkative. If they ever questioned their daughters' actions, the girls would threaten to take the grandchildren away. So these grandparents now take the kids to the dentist, enrol them in dance classes, go on field trips, and even play Santa. But they can't do the one thing they yearn to: protect the kids from the harm that comes from having a mother who doesn't want to love you.

We may look at these grandparents and say, "Cut her off!" But honestly, if you looked at the faces of the children, growing more jaded by the year, would it be that easy for you? It wouldn't for me. And yet, at some level, I wonder if that instinct is at least partially correct.

Sometimes the best thing we can do to our kids is to make them hurt for a while: to let them feel the consequences of their actions. Whether our kids are parents themselves or irresponsible adults running to us to bail them out once again, bailing is not helping. They can continue to wreck their lives, because they know we will always pick up the pieces.

Nevertheless, when small children are involved, bailing out is sometimes necessary, since you want to continue to see the grandchildren. But perhaps, if these children are no longer her free lunch, she will give you custody. (And if you do suspect that your child is taking your grandchildren into dangerous places, please call Children's Aid. It may cause a war in your family, but the children will be safe.)

Unfortunately none of this is a solution to a grandmother's tears: the tears of grief that a child you raised could do these things, and the tears of fear for the future. And making difficult decisions now, in the hopes that the situation will improve, will cause even more tears to flow. Let's hope, though, that these tears will usher in a change in the relationship, so that fewer tears will fall later.


# In Gratitude for Nana
*This column was first published April 28, 2003*

Most people love their mothers, but not everyone likes them. Mothers can annoy you, nag you, and give you a load of guilt that no one else is quite capable of. That's one of the reasons that I thank God every day for my own. We've had our ups and downs, but I can honestly say that my mother is my best friend. And we have fun together, too. We're both avid knitters, and now every month we get together with some other women to chat and to knit. Her mother taught her to knit, and her mother taught her, all the way back for generations. I still have some beautiful items knitted by my great-grandmother, and now we're starting to teach my oldest daughter to knit.

**And then the words came tumbling out. Breast cancer. Very advanced case.**

Perhaps the best thing about my mother is how much she loves my daughters. She moved to Belleville, away from all her friends, just so she could be a Nana. And the girls adore her. I cannot imagine their lives, or mine, without her.

And yet, half a lifetime ago, I did just that. I arrived home from a part-time job one afternoon when I was 16 to find my mother sitting shrivelled on the couch. She was all hunched up, with a box of Kleenex by her side, and when she saw me she tried to be brave. "Sheila, come sit down. We have to talk about something."

And then the words came tumbling out. Breast cancer. Very advanced case. Admitted tomorrow. Surgery in three days. There was a good chance this would be fatal. She was 43 years old.

I sat and struggled not to cry, knowing that my mother's concern was far more for me than for her. She knew where she was going; she was not afraid of death.

But it was just the two of us, and I was still young. She didn't want to leave me alone. Instead of *her* life passing before her eyes, my life did. All the things she wanted to see: my graduation, my wedding, my children. She wanted to know who I would become.

I then acted in a very 16-year-old fashion. I left my mother, shrivelled on the couch, and took the subway to a friend's house to talk. In retrospect, I wish I had stayed, not saying anything, and just hugged my mother.

The next few weeks were intense, as she had a very painful surgery and awaited tests. I walked down to the hospital between my high school classes to see her. Then, about a week and a half later, we had some astounding news. The cancer had not spread. The oncologist said he had never seen such an advanced case that surgery had cured. There was not even a need for follow-up treatment.

On the tenth year anniversary of her surgery, we took her out for dinner. I tried to find a "Glad You're Not Dead" card, but Hallmark didn't seem to make any, so I made one, and Rebecca coloured on it. During that evening she bounced Rebecca on her knee, and Keith and I celebrated together that our daughter had a Nana. Now Rebecca is 8, and is itching to learn to knit. Nana is ready, eager to heed the call.

Eighty years ago another 8-year-old learned to knit. My great-grandmother taught my grandmother, who took to it immediately. My grandmother, too, had a younger sister, just like Rebecca does. She loved Dorrie to pieces, and I'm sure they played house, and tea set, and school, and all the things my little girls do.

But Dorrie never learned to knit. During the days that my grandmother was attempting it, they were quarantined inside their house, because Dorrie had diphtheria. Unlike my mother, she didn't make it, and my grandmother never really recovered losing her best friend.

Rebecca will never face that with Katie. Katie will not get diphtheria, or measles, or even, please God, smallpox, because over the last 80 years we have figured out ways to cure them. Perhaps in the next few decades we will cure cancer, too, so that my girls will never have to contemplate losing their mother, or dying before they can teach their own granddaughters how to knit.

*This is one of the columns I'm most proud of. As I'm compiling this book, I'm about to take off for a four-day knitting conference with my mom in Atlantic City. Maybe one day, when my daughters are older, they'll come, too. Even if they don't, I'm glad Mom and I have this chance now, because not too many years ago I thought it would never happen.*

## In Defence of the "Wrongfully" Born

ow do you feel when someone insults your child? When a coach won't put him in the front lineup; when a teacher tells you your daughter's difficult; when a neighbour says she's funny looking? You probably want to take a swing at them!

Well, what if a judge decided that your child shouldn't have been born? That his life was a mistake? How would you feel then?

For 29 days I held a baby. I sang to him, I rocked

him, I kissed him. I loved him as fiercely as I have ever loved anyone in my life. And then I said goodbye when the doctor brought him to me after they couldn't revive him. Across the country, judges are ruling that babies like him can be considered "wrongfully born."

My son Christopher had Down Syndrome and a heart defect. We knew about it when I was 22 weeks pregnant. The most likely prognosis was that he would live for a few years but would eventually die prematurely. Unfortunately, his life was even shorter than the doctors originally predicted.

Recently a couple in Saskatchewan also had a child with Down Syndrome. Their daughter, though, survived. Evidently this was not their preferred outcome, since they sued the obstetrician for not giving them the opportunity to abort her in the first place. As angry as I feel at our legal system, I feel much sadder for this couple.

They are blessed with a child. That child will not be as intelligent as most children and will likely have more health problems. That child may have difficulty living independently and will be a source of concern over the years. But that child will also have more than the usual dose of generosity, compassion, and fun. She will love life. She will have a ready smile, and she will inspire one in those around her. Those born with Down Syndrome seem to have an extra "kindness" gene, for they are the flowers that bloom even in winter.

Yet this couple went to court because they believe she should not be here. Yes, having a child with birth defects is a tremendous disappointment; it's a shock that alters our goals, our dreams, and even our ideas of who we are. The parents that I know with disabled children, though, report that their children are blessings. They would not have planned it, but the situation has made them kinder people. They have learned that what matters in life is not so much our successes but our choices and attitudes along the way.

I hope and pray that this couple will one day see this. In the meantime, however, they are accelerating a fundamental change in our legal system that endangers us all. Where are we, as a society, if we believe "defects" renders one's right to life null and void? What if genetic testing could identify all birth defects so we could abort everyone who wasn't perfect? What would our attitude then be to our seniors with Alzheimer's, or to those with other debilitating illnesses? It seems that we are evolving into a culture that believes we have the right to tailor-make our babies, and in so doing we're losing our compassion for those who don't meet our high standards.

If I had one wish in life, it would be that I could hold Christopher once again on this side of heaven. I would whisper "I love you" enough to last until I can see him again. My most precious possession is a box with a lock of his hair, his pacifier, and his handprints and footprints that were taken after he died. Everyone knows if there's ever a fire, that's what I care about most.

Many may think I had it easy. I only had him for 29 days, and I didn't have to bear the burden of caring for him for the rest of his life. To a certain extent they may be right. But I would gladly bear that burden to hold him again. Those 29 days are the most precious of my life. I only hope that this couple can learn to love their daughter the way she is, too. We don't choose our children, but we can choose either to love them or resent them. I know what most Down Syndrome people would choose. As a society, what will we?

*I'm going to end this book with my favourite column. This is one that just came to me, with very little effort, and the e-mails I received in response to it were beautiful. People who had gone through tremendous grief, of all different kinds, wrote to say they were grateful to have it put in words like this. Little has touched me as much as a writer as the comments I received on this column. Without further adieu, I'll let it be my final words in this book.*

## A Prayer Through Tears
*This column was first published August 30, 2004*

In a few days I'll take my girls to the cemetery, for one of our regular visits on the anniversary of their brother's death. It's been eight years now, but the pain still hits when you least expect it.

Last week, in my hometown, another set of parents endured the unimaginable, this time because their seven-year-old drowned in a tragic accident. I'm sure, though, that they are not the only ones with fresh wounds. There are others who are grieving today: parents who have miscarried, or lost a baby like I did, or had accidents, whether or not it hit the news. Even if it happened long ago, such grief does not just evaporate. After my son died, I realized that one cannot comfort a grieving parent as one would like to, because there are no words. But one can listen, one can hug, and one can pray. And so I would like to share some of my thoughts and prayers for those of us who have entered this horrible fraternity of grieving parents, in the hopes that it may help some of you, too.

When a child dies it feels as if the physical laws of the universe have been violated. You needed that child far more than you need the very oxygen you breathe, and yet that child is gone, and your lungs keep working. Your very breath is a betrayal, and squeezes your chest worse than any violence ever could. So I pray that you will be able to take each breath, and that eventually simply living won't hurt like this any more.

And I pray that in your grief you and your spouse will be able to turn to each other. The death of a child strains a marriage in a way little else does. It's not fair, but you face a crossroads. I pray you will walk this valley together, and that the journey will strengthen you, rather than separate you.

I pray that people will surround you with practical help, that they will hug and that they will listen. I pray that your friends won't scatter because they feel awkward, but that they will be patient, even when the grief seems to be lasting longer than others think it should. I pray that if your grief is from a miscarriage or a stillbirth, people will still understand the depth of your pain.

I also pray that you will be able to take each day as it comes. When a child dies, and especially a baby who did not have the chance to become part of your daily routine, on the outside it is almost as if he or she never existed. And yet, for you that child was your very heart. If you let go of the grief, it is as if you are letting go of the last thing that ties you to your baby. Remember, though, that grief is not something that disappears. Sometimes grief is overt, but other times you feel fine. I pray that you will embrace those moments when you feel peace, because there will be moments—even if it's days, weeks, or years later—when the grief will return, unbidden, in full force. Be grateful for good days and do not feel guilty for them. Smiling is not betraying your child.

At the same time, I pray that when those good days become the norm, even if it's years down the road, that you will not feel like you are going crazy if the grief suddenly hits you hard again. You're not regressing, or starting at square one. This is the way of grief, and know that it never completely disappears. If we are honest, we probably wouldn't want it any other way. So I pray that in those moments when you can't breathe again, that you will still experience peace and know that this intensity will again subside.

I pray that you will remember that every day that passes is not one more day further away from your child but instead one more day that you are closer to meeting your baby again.

And finally, I pray that one day you will be able to remember with laughter, and not just with tears.

Amen.

*To Love, Honor, and Vacuum* will encourage you to deal with your hectic life by prioritizing relationships and fostering responsibility and respect in all family members. When you apply these real-world, real-life insights, you'll discover what it means to love and honor... in spite of the vacuuming.

"Sheila is about to challenge your thinking about your role as a wife and mother. I don't say that lightly. I read more advice about mothering and womanhood in a week than most people read in a year. But Sheila is on to something here."

—Carla Barnhill
Editor, *Christian Parenting Today*

"Reading this book provides a stimulus to do practical things to make life happier for everyone."

—*Christian Observer*

"Gregoire's enthusiasm, real-life examples, and emphasis on healthy relationships will encourage women."

—*CBA Marketplace*

"Gregoire recognizes that for many women, housework isn't just housework. It's a source of deep anxiety, stress, and friction, but it doesn't have to be that way. If housework is driving you insane, you aren't alone."

—*San Diego Family*

"*To Love, Honor, and Vacuum* is full of helpful, practical ideas any mom can use."

—*Living Light News*

*To Love, Honor, and Vacuum: When you feel more like a maid than a wife and mother.* Kregel Publications, 2003 0-8524-2699-5 17.50 CA/$11.99 US

It's 10:00 p.m.
He wants to start snuggling.
You want to start snoring.

He feels unloved because you aren't "in the mood," and you feel unloved because he only cares about one thing.

*Honey I Don't Have a Headache Tonight* helps you overcome this frustrating stalemate. This practical—and often humorous—book gives easy-to-follow advice on how to turn up the heat in your marriage when a solitary bubble bath seems much more enticing than your hubby waiting in the bedroom.

"Gregoire has produced a must-read book for all married couples and those planning to get married...[It] will have both husbands and wives nodding and laughing and saying, 'Yeah, that's right! That's just how it is!'"

—*Maranatha News*

"Sheila's wit allows her to successfully tackle a sensitive subject."

—Denise MacDonald, Marriage and Family Therapist

"In a refreshingly down-to-earth tone, Gregoire uses biblical principles and humor to show wives how to overcome their obstacles to desire."

—"Our Pick," *Today's Christian Woman*

"Women, if you want to REALLY understand your man's needs and expectations, this book is for you."

—David Murrow, Amazon.com

*Honey I Don't Have a Headache Tonight: Help for women who want to feel more in the mood.* Kregel Publications, 2004 0-8524-2693-6  15.99 CA/$10.99 US

# Sheila is available to speak at:

- Parenting conferences
- Community groups
- Church groups
- Women's retreats
- Marriage enrichment seminars
- Home-schooling conventions

Some of her topics include:

*Stop Doing Good Things—and do The Best!*
You may spend your life doing lots of lots of good things—and still feel like you're just walking in circles. It's likely because, though your life may be full of lots of good things, you're missing out on the best. Find out how we can start saying no to things that get us off track, and put our energies instead towards the things that make us truly happy and build strong families.

*Packing Your Kids' Baggage*
You often hear people saying "he left home with such baggage." They mean it as an insult. He left home with unresolved issues from his family, and they're affecting his relationships now. But all of us have baggage, whether good or bad. What are you doing today as a parent to ensure your kids grow up with the right baggage—and not the bad stuff?

*Stronger than Steel*
We all want great marriages, but they don't just happen. Too many things conspire to pull us apart from

each other: toddlers' demands, sleepless nights, busy work schedules, impossibly hectic school schedules. Yet a good marriage is the foundation on which everything else in the family is built. Find out how you can grow your marriage so it's stronger than steel—and none of these outside influences can pull it apart.

*All in the Family*
Look at the newspapers today and you'll read story after story of heartache, evil, corruption, and violence. But where does it all begin? And where does it all end? This seminar takes listeners through the evolution of the family unit over the last few centuries and shows how changes in the family are causing society to shift. Find out why we're experiencing some of the societal changes we are today, what's likely to happen in the future, and how we can do our part to make sure children continue to grow up loved, cherished, and prepared for adulthood.

*To Love, Honour and Vacuum*
If you're a mom, you're likely exhausted. And if you're exhausted, you probably need a break! This seminar gives moms the hope and encouragement they need, while pointing them on the right road to more rest and better relationships as they raise their children. It will help harried women organize and prioritize, while providing lots of laughs along the way!

*You can find more of Sheila's topics, and how to book her for speaking engagements, at www.SheilaWrayGregoire.com*

# Get in Touch with Sheila

Want to send Sheila an e-mail?
Comment on one of her columns?
Find out about her speaking engagements
or about what else she's written?

You can find her at
www.SheilaWrayGregoire.com

or at

Box 20201
Belleville, ON  Canada
K8N 5V1